COASTAL & OCEAN SEAMANSHIP

Reed's
YACHT MASTER
Series

COASTAL & OCEAN
SEAMANSHIP

Edited by Capt. Oswald M. Watts,
Master Mariner, F.R.A.S., F.I.N.,
Editor of Reed's Nautical Almanac

THOMAS REED PUBLICATIONS LIMITED

First edition—1971

In the same series:

Coastal Navigation
Meteorology
Radar in Small Craft
Ocean Navigation

©

Published in Great Britain by Thomas Reed Publications Limited
and printed by Thomas Reed and Company Limited,
Sunderland, London and Glasgow.

Preface

It has been said that navigation is the art of finding one's way from one place to another but seamanship is the art of getting there.

It follows that the aim should be to get there safely without damage to life or ship. Yachtsmen entering for the Department of Trade & Industry examinations should remember that the emphasis will be on SAFETY and whilst it is important to know the Rules and Regulations applicable to yachts it is perhaps more important to be able to apply them. The knowledge that a yacht of a certain size must have a fire extinguisher of a certain type is not sufficient; it must also be known that that extinguisher is only efficient on a particular kind of fire and perhaps more important, how to set it off. Similarly, one should know how to fire the distress rockets purchased at some expense and not wait to try and read the instructions when dismasted and baling in the middle of the Channel on a wet dark night. Although it is not a requirement that the Regulations for the Prevention of Collision at Sea be learned by heart one may derive much advantage from doing so. The syllabus of the Examination calls for a full knowledge of the content and application of the Regulations. The initial definitions are very important as are the positions and ranges of lights and shapes. A yachtsman off the coast of the United Kingdom is likely to meet some of the less usual navigation light patterns more often than the deep sea man who seldom ventures into shoal water without a Pilot. He should be prepared to deal with the surprise situation. Similarly, a yachtsman must appreciate the difficulties of long deep draughted vessels offering large windage in tidal waters and narrow channels and so learn that there are situations when he might be considered a nuisance and should keep well clear.

The Rule of the Road is perhaps the most important part of a Yachtmasters' oral examination; one or more serious mistakes may bring failure whereas this may not be the case in other sections of the syllabus. The oral examination in Seamanship may take up to an hour or more. A great deal depends upon your reactions being quick, decisive and positive, as indeed they need to be at the helm of a yacht. In giving an answer be prepared, if asked, to back it up with a reason. The Department of Trade & Industry Examiners are all experienced Shipmasters. They are wise in the ways of the sea and know that very often there are more ways than one of doing something. A clear and reasoned answer will receive a fair hearing even if it is not quite the way the Examiner would do it himself.

It is hoped, that after studying the contents of this book, you will have sufficient knowledge to cope with the examination; if you have been able to put your knowledge to the test at sea so much the better. There is no school equal to practical experience.

O.M.W.

Acknowledgements

This book has been written to cover as concisely as possible, the Seamanship requirements of yachtsmen in general and those taking the Yacht Master Certificates in particular. Both sea-going Master Mariners and Yachtsmen have participated in its production.

Among the latter I would like to express my appreciation to Arthur Somers for his excellent work and sketches on the two chapters dealing with The Handling of Yachts —in Harbour and at Sea.

I should also like to thank Captain John Williams who prepared the Merchant Shipping and Admiralty Notices to Mariners, David Bartlett for his work on the Collision Regulations and the Department of Trade and Industry for kind permission to reproduce the photographs of the rocket life-saving apparatus and sketches of landing signals etc. in the Lifesaving Chapter.

I am greatly indebted to the marine staff of The Pyrene Company Limited who greatly assisted with the Chapter on Fire and kindly supplied the illustrations.

My final thanks must go to Jean Fowler, who sorted out all the copy, lettered the diagrams, translated the many hieroglyphics and finally prepared the manuscript for press.

O.M.W.

Contents

Chapter One

Ropes and Rigging

STANDING RIGGING

This is made up of all the ropes which are permanently fitted and secured in a boat.
The forestay is a rope leading from the upper part of the mast to the bows. Its purpose is to prevent the mast from falling aft.
A backstay is a rope which leads aft from the masthead to prevent the mast from falling forward.
Shrouds are ropes led from the masthead to the sides of the boat abreast the mast, they support the mast athwartships. There may be more than one on each side.
In modern boats the standing rigging is made of stainless or galvanised wire.

RUNNING RIGGING

This is made up of all ropes which can be moved such as halyards, sheets and topping lifts.
A halyard is a rope made fast in such a way that the boat's sail can be hoisted and lowered under control.
A sheet is a rope bent to the clew of the sail and is used for trimming the sail. In small boats it is never made fast at its other end. The helmsman or crew usually holds the end having taken a turn round a cleat. It can then be "let fly" to spill the wind out of the sail should a sudden squall catch him unawares. In large boats the sheet is hardened in on a sheet winch and then made fast.
A topping lift is a special kind of halyard used for adjusting the unfixed end of a boom or gaff.
Any item of running rigging may be found in the form of a purchase.

BLOCKS   See Fig. 1.1

A block is a portable pulley through which a rope may be rove.
The parts may be of wood, metal or a combination of the two. They consist of the body known as the shell; the sheave, which is a grooved wheel over which a rope may run; the pin, on which the sheave rotates; and the fitting for securing the block in its position which may be an eye, hook or strop.
The opening between the upper edge of the sheave and the shell through which the rope is passed is known as the swallow. The side of the shell is known as the cheek.
Wooden blocks are grouped by their size which is the length measured along the shell from top to bottom.

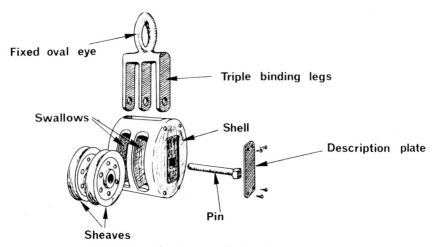

Fixed oval eye

Triple binding legs

Swallows

Shell

Description plate

Pin

Sheaves

Fig. 1.1   A wooden block and its parts

A rope requires an ordinary wooden block three times its size when a rope is classed by its circumference, e.g. a 2 inch rope requires a 6 inch block.

Metal blocks are grouped by the rope size for which they are designed and this is usually marked on the description plate.

Blocks may have more than one sheave and are described as single, double, treble blocks and so on.

A snatch block is a single block in which part of the shell is hinged to allow a bight of rope to be inserted into the swallow from one side. It is much weaker, size for size, than an ordinary block.

The Safe Working Load of a block should be marked on it and is the maximum weight of hoist for which the block should be used.

PURCHASES AND TACKLES

A purchase is a mechanical device by means of which an applied pull may be increased in value.

A tackle is a purchase. It consists of a rope rove through two or more blocks so that the value of any pull on the hauling part is increased. The amount of increase depends upon the number of sheaves in the blocks and how the rope is rove through them. Its size is known by the size of its fall.

A two block tackle in use consists of a standing or fixed block and a moving block. The rope, or fall, rove through the blocks has its hauling, standing and running parts.

The value by which the pull imparted to the hauling part is increased is known as the mechanical advantage, and disregarding friction this will be equal to the number of parts of rope at the moving block.

A tackle is rove to advantage when the number of parts of rope at the moving block exceeds the number at the standing block, and to disadvantage when vice versa.

A dinghy halyard is an example of the Single Whip; a fall rove through a single standing block. No mechanical advantage is gained.

In a larger boat the boom topping lift may be a Double Whip, i.e. a purchase used for hoisting. It consists of two single blocks with the standing part made fast to the upper block. It is usually rove to disadvantage and then has a mechanical advantage of two.

A Gun Tackle consists of two single blocks but is not used for hoisting. A boat's main sheet may be a gun tackle rove to advantage in which case the mechanical advantage is three.

A Luff Tackle has a double and a single block with the standing part on the single block and is usually a tackle of three inches or more in size.

A Handy Billy is a small tackle of less than two inches in size, it is usually rove as a luff or jigger tackle.

Two fold purchases have two double blocks.

Three fold purchases have two treble blocks.

CORDAGE

Cordage is rope made of vegetable fibres.
Each vegetable fibre may be only four or five feet long and in the manufacture of rope the first process is combing, in which the fibres are combed out into a long even ribbon. The ribbons are then spun into yarns and the twist binds the fibres together. The yarns may be spun left or right handed.

A strand is formed by twisting a number of yarns together either left or right handed but opposite to the spin of the yarns.

A number of strands are now layed up into a rope. The direction of lay will be opposite to the twist in the strands.

Three strands laid up make a "hawser laid rope." Four strands laid up round a heart makes a "shroud laid" rope less liable to stretch.

Three "hawser laid" ropes laid up in a direction opposite to their own lay make a "cable or water laid" rope which has more elasticity than a "hawser laid" rope of the same size but is not as strong; it is, however, more chafe resistant and does not absorb water so readily.

Cordage is one of the most used items in a boat and serves many purposes, e.g. running rigging, moorings, servings, seizing, caulking, leadlines, lashings, stoppers.
Fibres used in the manufacture of rope are usually of four kinds.

Manilla. This is a fibre from the leaf of the wild banana tree grown in the Philippines. It is flexible and stands weather and wear very well. It is usually used for lifting gear where a failure might cause danger to the crew.

Sisal. Made from the leaf of the agave grown in East Africa. As rope it is not as reliable as manilla and should only be used for general purposes.

Hemp. Comes from the skin of a nettle type plant grown in many parts of the world. It is softer to the touch than other fibres and Italian hemp is the strongest of rope fibres. It is usually used only for small lines and small stuff in the United Kingdom.

Coir is made from the husk fibres of coconuts. It is the weakest of the fibres but is very light and will float. It is very flexible and springy but will rot quickly if left wet.

Cordage of less than $\frac{1}{2}$ inch circumference is called small stuff.

Twines—two, three or four threads twisted together. Used for whipping and canvas sewing.

Spunyarn—similar to twine but much larger. Used for serving.

Marline—yarns which are laid up, not twisted together as in spunyarn. Used for small stops and similar work, also for marling down.

CARE OF ROPES

All ropes in a boat must be inspected for wear and condition at frequent intervals. If it has been necessary to stow a wet rope it should be brought out and dried as soon as possible. Keep all ropes free of kinks. Right handed ropes should be coiled down clockwise. Protect your ropes from chafe, e.g. the part of a halyard which is in a block when the sail is hoisted is particularly liable to chafe and this part should be tightly parcelled. All running rigging should be end for ended regularly, as should ropes used for mooring and anchor work.

BENDS AND HITCHES

Bends are used, generally, for joining the ends of two ropes together.
Hitches are used for securing a rope to another object.
A Knot is the interlacement of a single rope or of its strands.

The making of bends, hitches and knots should be practised frequently. Two short lengths of codline, or even string, may be carried in the pocket and used for practice at odd moments in the course of daily life. Only practice will bring expertise and deftness when working with rope. Yachtsmen should find the following sufficient for most requirements. See Fig. 1.2.

(1) A round turn and two half hitches.
This will never jamb and may be cast off quickly. Used for securing the painter to a mooring ring. If left untended the end should be stopped to the standing part.

(2) Clove hitch—used for securing to a rail or spar. If pulled sideways it will move along. It may be made with an end or bight of rope.

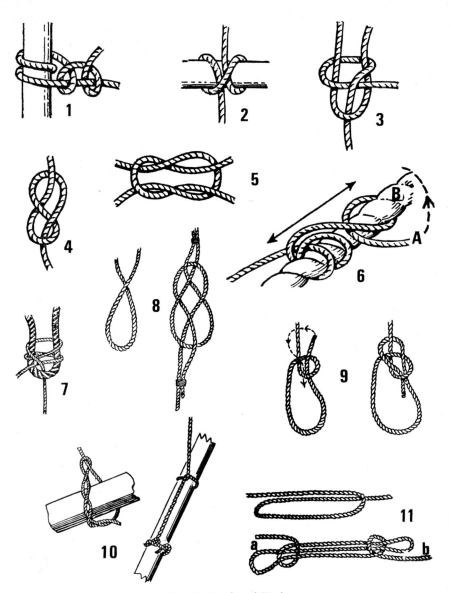

Fig. 1.2   Bends and Hitches

(3) Sheet bend—for bending a small rope to the eye of another, or the jib halyard to the peak of the jib.

(4) The figure of eight knot—put into the end of a rope to prevent it coming out of a block. Used in the logline for securing the rotator.

(5) Reef knot—for tying reef points, it consists of two overhand knots but the ends are crossed opposite ways each time. If they are crossed the same way, the result is a "granny" which may slip or jamb or come undone of its own accord when there is no strain on it.

(6) Rolling Hitch—it will not slip when a pull is exerted from one side. Used for securing a rope to a spar to be moved, or tailing a small block on to a larger rope.

(7) Double Sheet Bend—it has more security than the sheet bend as the end is rove twice. Used to make a gantline fast to the Bosun's Chair.

(8) Carrick Bend—the ends should be stopped to their standing parts. Used to join two hawsers together, especially if the join has to pass over a winch drum.

(9) Bowline knot—very reliable and will not slip. Makes a temporary eye in the end of a rope. Can be made using one hand only after practice.

(10) Timber hitch—for securing a rope's end when lifting a bale or spar. The turns should always be made with the lay of the rope. For hoisting, lowering or towing a spar a further half hitch should be made on the hauling side which should be towards the thicker end of the spar.

(11) Sheepshank—for shortening a rope temporarily. The loops should be stopped at points "A" and "B" in Figure 1.2.11.

It should be kept in mind that, in that portion of a rope where a knot, bend or hitch is made, the strength of that rope may be reduced by up to 60 per cent.

WHIPPING

The end of a rope will become unlaid and frayed if not secured in some way. In order to stop this happening the rope should be whipped with twine. The Common Whipping is illustrated in Figure 1.3.

Lay one end of your twine along the rope, "D" in Figure. Take about eight turns tightly around the rope against the lay, covering the end of twine as well. Holding these turns with the thumb lay the other end of the twine, "BC" in Figure, along the rope in the opposite direction to "D" and over the turns already made, making sure that you leave a bight in the twine at "A". Now take the part of the bight at "A" and pass it in turns over part "B" until the loop at "E" is small. Now pull tight at "C" and cut off the loose end. If it is desired to put a whipping on a bight of rope, it can be done in a similar manner except that to finish you take the last three or four turns over one finger held against the rope and pass the end of the twine back through them. Now remove the finger, work the loose ends taut, heave tight and cut off the loose end.

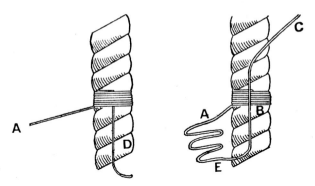

Fig. 1.3   Common Whipping

MOUSING

A mousing is put across the mouth of a hook to prevent it from becoming unhooked, and is usually made with seizing wire if it is likely to receive any chafe. A bight of the wire is held at the back of the hook and the two ends passed round and through the bight. It is then hauled taut and caught round the bill of the hook. A number of turns are passed around the back and bill with the two ends together. The ends are then separated and one is wrapped around the turns already made thus binding them together. The mousing is finished off securely by tying the two ends together.

If a permanent mousing is not required, pass a few turns of spun yarn around from the bill to the back of the hook and bind them tightly together.

MOORING LINES AND STOPPERS

The size of mooring lines will depend on the size of the yacht but generally there will be head and stern lines, breast lines and springs. When these lines are on deck always keep them coiled down and clear of metalwork. Never allow kinks to form in your ropes. If they do, the best way of removing them may be to tow the rope over the stern at a convenient time. When stowing your ropes away at sea put your fenders, heaving line and any stoppers on top of them so as to be readily available.

To transfer a rope with weight on it from a winch to bitts it is necessary to "stopper" it off while making the transfer. Figure 1.4 illustrates this. It will be seen that, the stopper or smaller rope having had one end made fast to a strong point, is applied to the larger rope in the form of a rolling hitch against the lay, but instead of a further half hitch the end is backed round the rope in the lay and the end held. If mooring lines are synthetic then a synthetic stopper should be used.

Fig. 1.4   Rope stopper on rope

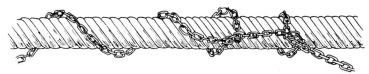

Fig 1.4a Chain stopper on wire

If it is desired to stopper off a wire, a chain is used, as rope cannot grip the wire properly. A widely spaced "cow hitch" is formed with the chain and the end backed round the wire. If two continuing half hitches are used they are liable to jamb after slipping together. Fig. 1.4a

The chain stopper may be used for holding the weight on a mooring wire while the hauling part is taken to the winch drum for heaving taut. It may be used on a wire halyard or topping lift for the same purpose.

SPLICING

The rope eye splice, Figure 1.5, is a means of forming a soft eye in the end of a rope, such as is found in moorings for dropping over bitts or a mooring bollard.

Unlay the end of the rope to be spliced for a sufficient length to make a little more than 3 tucks through the lay. Now form an eye with the unlaid end on top. To form the first tuck, take the middle end and tuck it underneath a strand in the standing part from right to left. To make the second tuck pick up the left hand end and pass it over the strand with the middle end under it and tuck it under the next strand to the left on the standing part. For the third tuck turn the splice over. Take the third end and pass it over the third strand from left to right, then tuck it underneath the latter from right to left. An end should now be coming out from under each of three consecutive strands. To make a second and third round of tucks, each end is now led over one strand and under the next. To tidy the ends do an extra round of tucks with halved strands. The strands should be halved on the underside so that the cut ends are hidden.

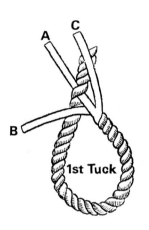 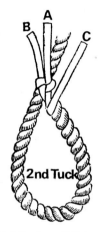 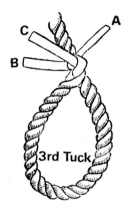

Fig. 1.5   Rope Splicing

The *Short Splice* is used for joining together the ends of two ropes of the same size when it is not required that the splice pass through a block. Unlay the two ends to be joined for a length equal to the number of tucks decided upon. Marry the two ends together strand for strand, i.e. so that no two strands in the same end are next to each other. Now, make the first tuck in each of the ends by passing each of the three strands in one part over one strand and under the next in the other part. Having done this, ensure there are no kinks and that each end is running smoothly over and under a strand. The second and third tucks in each part should now be made in the same manner.

The *Long Splice* is used when the rope has to pass through a block. It is wasteful of rope and only considered to be a temporary measure. Unlay the ends about four times as much as for a short splice and marry them together as if about to commence the latter. Instead of tucking, choose two ends opposite to each other, unlay one of them for two or more feet, laying the opposite one into its place.
Take two more opposite strands and repeat but in the opposite direction.
The third pair of strands are left alone, so that there are now three pairs of ends. Make an overhand knot in the lay with each pair, pull tight, halve the strands and tuck over one and under one, halve again and tuck to taper off.

The *Back Splice* is an alternative to whipping the end of a rope.
Unlay the end of the rope, form a crown by interlacing the ends of the strands so that each end is pointing down the rope when the crown is pulled tight. Now tuck each of the strands over one and under one back down the standing part.

SYNTHETIC ROPES

Recommendations for selection, use and care of man-made fibre ropes in marine applications are laid down in British Standard No. 4128 of 1967.
Synthetic fibre ropes give little warning before breaking. Stretch can be up to double that of fibre ropes when in tension and if released such a rope acts like an elastic band with great recoil action on breaking.
These ropes have high strength in tension and are very durable. They do not rot or mildew and absorb very little water. However, they have a low melting point and frictional heat on a winch drum can tend to fuse the turns. The low melting point is turned to advantage in finishing off ends. The strand ends can be fused together with heat thus avoiding the necessity for whipping.
Never expose to sunlight more than is necessary. Cover with canvas or stow away. Keep clear of all chemicals, paint, and heat sources. Proprietary rust removers are particularly injurious to synthetic ropes.
Synthetic ropes should be inspected for wear internally and externally. A high degree of powdering will be seen between the strands of a rope which has had excessive wear and its strength will be much reduced. The more the stretch in the nature of the man-made fibre the rope is made of, the more will be the interstrand wear. Some nylon ropes become hard and stiff after being overworked.

WIRE SPLICING

Flexible steel wire rope is six stranded, right hand lay, and each strand has a hempen heart.
Put a stop on the wire at the place to which it is intended to unlay the strands. Whip the end of each strand.
Always make tucks with the lay. Use a long tapering spike and after inserting it under a strand do not take it out until the tuck is completed by pulling through all the slack of the strand.
To make an eye splice pass the first of the six strands through the centre of the standing part of the rope but not too close to the stop. Pass the next strand under two strands and the third strand under one strand. You are now left with three strands which should be taken to the back of the standing part and each in its turn passed under one strand. Each strand should now be tucked with the lay over and under the strand from under which it emerged at the first tuck. Five tucks should be made but at the fourth tuck the heart of each strand and half its wires may be cut out and at the fifth tuck the wires may be halved again in order to taper the splice.

BREAKING STRESS OF ROPE

The following breaking strains are in Tonnes where the Diameters "D" are in millimetres.

An adequate Safe Working Load may be assessed by dividing the breaking stress by six. Any rope obtained for use which is of different material or made up in another manner may have a greater or lesser breaking stress. Details should be obtained from the supplier.

METRIC FORMULAE

Flexible steel Wire Rope

Make up	*Breaking Stress*
12 wires in each of 6 strands	$\dfrac{15}{500} D^2$
24 wires in each of 6 strands	$\dfrac{20}{500} D^2$
37 wires in each of 6 strands	$\dfrac{21}{500} D^2$

Hawser Laid 3 stranded Fibre Rope

Manilla	$\dfrac{2}{300} D^2$
Polythene and Polypropylene	$\dfrac{3}{300} D^2$
Terylene	$\dfrac{4}{300} D^2$
Nylon	$\dfrac{5}{300} D^2$

SOUNDING LINES

To navigate safely it is necessary to know the depth of water in which one's vessel is afloat. The method of finding this out is called "sounding". Soundings are taken with a lead and line by "heaving the lead". This is achieved by attaching a lead to a line and dropping it overside when the vessel is stopped or heaving it ahead when the vessel is moving. The aim is to have the line "up and down" when the lead touches the sea bed. Note is taken of where the water surface cuts the line and thus the depth is known by means of the marks on the line.

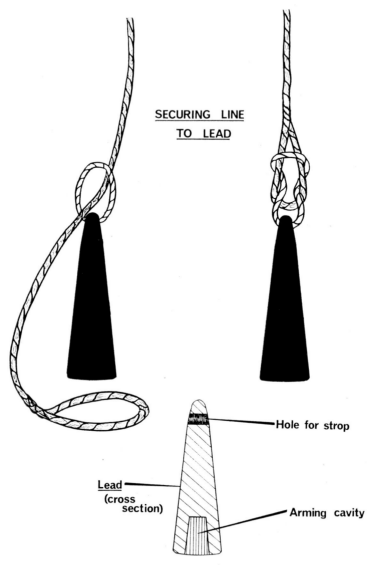

SECURING LINE
TO LEAD

Hole for strop

Lead
(cross
section)

Arming cavity

Fig. 1.6   Hand Lead

The Hand Lead is illustrated in Figure 1.6. It is used for sounding in depths up to 20 fathoms. The lead consists of a piece of bar lead tapered, weighing about 14 pounds. The base has a hollow in it to which may be applied an "arming" of white lead and tallow to obtain a sample of the sea bed. A hide becket or strop is usually rove through a hole or eye at the head of the lead. The lead-line has a soft eye at one end and to attach it to the lead it is rove through the head strop, the lead itself then being passed through the eye. When drawn together the hitch formed is called a "cow hitch".

The line is marked off as follows:

At 2 fathoms	—	two strips of leather.
3 fathoms	—	three strips of leather.
5 & 15 fathoms	—	a piece of white linen or duck canvas.
7 & 17 fathoms	—	a piece of red bunting.
10 fathoms	—	a piece of leather with a hole in it.
13 fathoms	—	a piece of blue serge
20 fathoms	—	a cord with two knots in it.

The first fathom does not include the length of the lead, thus in any sounding obtained there is a depth of water of that much additional to the report. This is known as the "benefit of the lead".

The marks on the line are made of different materials so that in the dark they may be distinguished by their feel on the fingers or lips.

The fathom soundings marked are called "marks". Those unmarked are called "deeps". In calling the soundings the fathom is always called last for the benefit of the navigator's or Pilot's ear.

Examples are:

6 fathoms	—	By the deep six
$6\frac{1}{4}$ fathoms	—	and a quarter six
$6\frac{1}{2}$ fathoms	—	and a half six
$6\frac{3}{4}$ fathoms	—	a quarter less seven
7 fathoms	—	by the mark seven.

The lead line may be dropped overside when at anchor in fog and if watched and felt can give an indication of the vessel dragging.

Small craft may like to use a smaller line in which case that illustrated in Figure 1.7 may be useful.

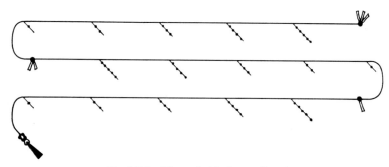

Fig. 1.7 lead line suitable for small craft

The lead should weigh about seven pounds. Mark the first three fathoms with one, two and three strips of material and divide each fathom into feet, marking with a cord with one to five knots in it as appropriate.

Chapter Two

Sailing Yachts—
Handling in Harbour

There are two situations where a good knowledge of the handling qualities of one's boat are important to the cruising man—the first is in harbour, using this term incidentally, to cover all situations where anchoring, mooring or tying up alongside are required. The second situation is at sea in heavy weather conditions where a knowledge of the characteristics of one's craft may make all the difference between arriving safely at the destination or becoming the object of an air/sea rescue operation. In this chapter we are concerned with the former situation and no apology is made for dealing in some detail with the fundamentals—observation of the strange manoeuvres of some sailing craft when carrying out comparatively simple procedures such as anchoring in a tideway indicate that the owners are still uncertain of some fairly basic seamanship. In the next two sections we shall deal with anchoring and mooring and, for the sake of simplicity, all anchor drill is assumed to be carried out with the auxiliary engine and all mooring work under sail. The principles of handling under sail as explained in the mooring section are equally applicable to anchoring under sail.

ANCHORING Fig 2.1

There are several points to consider when the decision to anchor has to be made. Dealing first with the situation in which the vessel will not be left unattended and will not be at anchor for more than one tide—in this situation it is a simple matter to pick a location where the anchor can be dropped in a suitable depth of water and there is adequate room for the vessel to drop back on the tide, keeping clear of all obstructions and other vessels. In the unusual case of anchoring in slack water with no wind it is important to remember to move astern as soon as the anchor has been dropped, in order to get it to bite, and also to avoid the possibility of piling all the chain neatly on top of the anchor, with possibly unfortunate results when the tidal stream starts to flow.

Length of anchor chain or warp

The golden rule when anchoring is to veer out a length of chain equal to three times the depth of high water at the particular location, this three-times rule applies to chain only. If a nylon warp is being used, the length should be five times the maximum depth and it is rather important to ensure that there is at least a couple of fathoms of chain shackled on to the anchor. This serves a two-fold purpose. Firstly, due to the weight it ensures there is a reasonably horizontal pull on the anchor which would probably not occur if the nylon warp was directly attached and, secondly, the presence of the chain at this particular point will reduce the chafe that would occur on a nylon warp lying on the sea bed. Whilst on the subject of the anchor and the anchor cable generally, it is perhaps worth mentioning that the inboard end of the cable should never be shackled below decks. It should always be secured with a fairly strong lashing which could, in an emergency, be cut. For example, a much larger vessel is seen drifting out of control towards one's own vessel. To weigh anchor would take too long, to cut a lashing and slip the chain is a quick and effective method of getting away smartly.

Buoying the anchor

In the previous paragraph the desirability is mentioned of being able to slip the anchor chain in conditions of emergency. To slip the cable without any ready means of recovery can be an expensive matter and it is a seamanlike precaution to buoy the anchor. The buoy rope is a light but strong line attached to the crown of the anchor with a small buoy preferably marked "anchor buoy" (cases have been known where an anchor buoy has been picked up under the mistaken impression that it was a mooring buoy). Buoying the anchor is also a prudent action if there is any doubt about the state of the bottom. If, for example, the latter is liable to be fouled with old moorings it is a wise precaution to buoy the anchor, securing the buoy line on to its crown. If it does foul, it may be possible to trip the anchor by hauling on the buoy rope. If it is impossible to recover the anchor and it is necessary to slip it, at least the anchor is clearly marked for future recovery operations.

Indication when at anchor

A final point and one rarely observed by owners of small yachts, is the necessity for indicating that the vessel is anchored. Collision regulations require a black ball or similar shape to be suspended at the fore part of the vessel; in the case of a small yacht this would be on the forestay. It may perhaps seem unnecessary to carry out this sort of drill but it should be realised that when anchoring close to a busy fairway it may be of great help to commercial craft operating under possibly difficult conditions. Quite apart from this, should one be unfortunate enough to be run down it is a consoling thought to know that when dealing with the insurance company one can at least affirm that the correct signals were being properly displayed at the time. After sunset the black ball will be replaced with a white light.

Anchoring for more than one tide

Having considered some of the fundamental aspects of anchoring the situation can now be considered in which a vessel is to be anchored for more than one tide. When it is known that the vessel will be left for more than a tide, the most important point to observe in addition to those already mentioned, is the area available for swinging. For example, if one is anchored in water with a maximum depth of say 30 feet this means that there will be at least 90 feet of chain out and the vessel will probably be about 60 feet from her anchor in a horizontal plane. When the tide changes the vessel will swing through a distance of approx. 120 feet and this must be allowed for when anchoring in the vicinity of moorings, obstructions, etc. In certain circumstances it may be considered prudent to restrict this swing at the turn of the tide by anchoring with a bower and kedge anchor, as shown in Fig. 2.2. Anchored in this manner it is

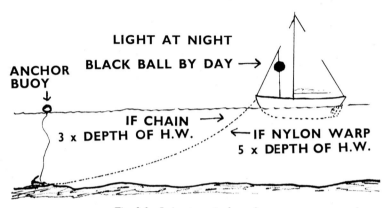

Fig. 2.1 Lying to a single anchor

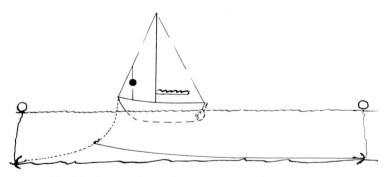

Fig. 2.2 Lying to bow and kedge anchors—kedge warp to be lowered to sufficient depth to avoid fouling passing vessels

clear that the vessel will ride to each anchor in turn and thereby considerably reduce the swinging area, at the same time eliminating the wandering caused by a single anchor tripping at each turn of tide. It is preferable to lay the bower anchor upstream so that the vessel lies to the heavier anchor on the faster ebb stream and the kedge anchor on the flood. The anchor drill in this situation is fairly easy to carry out, particularly if a dinghy is available. In these circumstances it is usual to drop the bower anchor first and then run the kedge out in the dinghy. If this is not available, the operation can be carried out by dropping the kedge on the run-up, then dropping the bower anchor and middling between the two. The kedge warp is then made fast on the bower anchor chain, using a rolling hitch for this, and the chain veered so that the kedge warp is well below the surface, as shown in Figure 2.2. Finally, it is worth remembering that if it is necessary to lie to a single anchor for several tides a slight sheer put on the helm will ensure that at the turn of the tide the vessel will swing clear of her anchor and not foul it.

TYPES OF MOORINGS

Securing to a buoy is a reasonably simple operation but it does involve the rather more difficult one of stopping the vessel immediately adjacent to the buoy in order that the buoy rope can be picked up and secured before wind and tide have started to move the vessel again.

Before considering the operation of securing to the buoy, it is perhaps worth noting the two methods commonly used these days for anchoring the buoys, for reasons which will be obvious if Figs. 2.3 and 2.4 are studied. In Fig. 2.3 it will be noted that there is a long length of ground chain secured to an anchor each end. In the middle of this there is a swivel to which is attached a third length of chain at the end of which is the buoy rope. The buoy being a fairly small one normally only supports the weight of

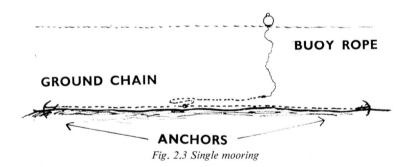

BUOY ROPE

GROUND CHAIN

ANCHORS

Fig. 2.3 Single mooring

the line which is attached to the end of the middle chain. It will be obvious that when this buoy is picked up there is sufficient slack before the chain is hauled aboard for the vessel to surge ahead for a short distance which may be useful if the conditions under which the buoy is being picked up are a little difficult. Having picked up the buoy the long rope is then hauled inboard until the chain is reached and made fast around the bitts or samson post.

In Fig. 2.4 the modern method of mooring is shown. In these days of congestion this type is rapidly superseding single mooring, being more economical of ground tackle and, even more important, of space. It will be seen that a number of buoys, in this case three, are secured to one ground mooring scope. Each buoy is much larger than the type previously mentioned and supports the weight of the single mooring chain. It will be seen that the length of the chain is little more than the depth at high water springs. The buoy is not brought inboard but the buoy rope, usually about two fathoms of stout rope secured to the buoy ring is brought inboard and made fast round the samson post. It is worth remembering that when securing to this type of

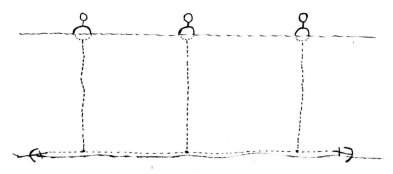

Fig. 2.4   Trot mooring

buoy, particularly at high water, the buoy will not move very much in a horizontal plane, thus it is important that the vessel should be almost stationary when the buoy rope is picked up. This lack of movement of the buoy is one of the main reasons for the use of this type of mooring—it permits a much greater number of vessels to be packed into a given area.

PICKING UP THE MOORING

When considering the drill for securing to a buoy, or anchoring, there are three standard situations—wind and tide together, wind against tide and wind across tide. It need hardly be said that with varying strengths of wind in relation to tidal strengths there are endless variations on any one theme.

Wind against tide

Examining first the wind against tide situation in which the vessel is approaching the buoy from the up tide position, the point to remember is that when sail is removed or reduced, the tidal effect on the hull becomes more effective and, it is therefore important that the tide should be used as the stopping influence. In these circumstances the vessel should make the final approach run to the buoy from the down tide position, see Fig. 2.5. If, however, the wind is so strong that the vessel will continue to be wind rode even with no sail up, then the approach should be made into the wind. Referring again to Fig. 2.5, the approach here, assuming moderate wind force, would be to tack up wind past the buoy, round up, drop mainsail and then run back over the tide under the foresail only, dropping this when it is apparent that the vessel is carrying sufficient way to reach the buoy.

If in tacking to the up wind position of the buoy a large Genoa is being carried, it may be more prudent to round up, drop the Genoa and then drop the main about halfway, securing it in this position with shock cord ties, see Fig. 2.6. This very much reduced mainsail can then be easily dropped and secured just before reaching the buoy.

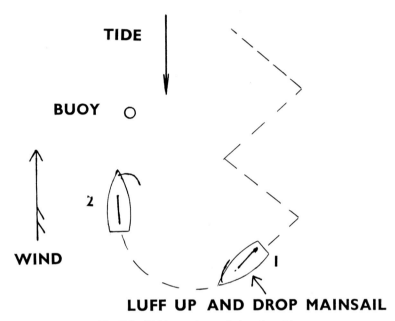

Fig. 2.5   *Picking up buoy wind against tide*

Wind and tide together

Considering now the case of wind and tide together, see Fig. 2.7. It will be necessary to tack up to the buoy, in all probability carrying full sail up to the moment of picking up the buoy. The aim should be to complete the final tack, rounding up into the wind at the buoy, or rather just below it; dependent on the strength of the wind and tide the rounding up should be made at a sufficient distance from the buoy to allow the vessel's way to be stopped by the time she reaches the buoy. In circumstances such as this it is better to err on the side of too much speed rather than too little as if the buoy is overshot the wind and tide will quickly bring the boat stern first back to the buoy, when it can be secured in passing. If there is insufficient way, the vessel may stop before reaching the buoy, necessitating paying off and making a fresh attempt. In crowded surroundings this may be a little difficult or possibly even dangerous. A useful gadget to have on board these days is a patent snap hook of which there are several varieties available.

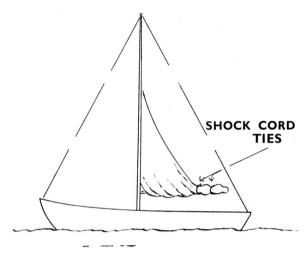

Fig. 2.6 The use of sail ties

This is attached to a short length of suitable line and used from the end of the boat hook. It is snapped on to the buoy ring as the vessel stops; the line should be strong enough to hold the vessel for the comparatively short time required to drop sail and generally secure; the snap hook line is then replaced with the permanent mooring line.

Tide and wind at 90°

Coming now to the third main combination of circumstances, wind at right angles to the tide, this is probably the easier situation to deal with, see Fig. 2.8. The vessel is able to stem the tide with the wind on the beam and run up to the buoy, let fly all sheets and moor. Alternatively and, perhaps to be preferred, the vessel can round up down tide of the buoy but to windward, the mainsail is dropped and the vessel moves slowly up to the buoy under foresail, as shown in B Fig. 2.8.

The three situations considered are the basic ones but as mentioned there are endless variations on any one theme, knowledge and experience will be needed to size up a situation and quickly decide the correct combinations of sails and angle of approach.

Speed of approach

There are, however, one or two important aspects relating to the problem of mooring that are worth bearing in mind. Firstly, it is usually possible to control the speed of the vessel under sail so that the actual operation of picking up the mooring can be carried

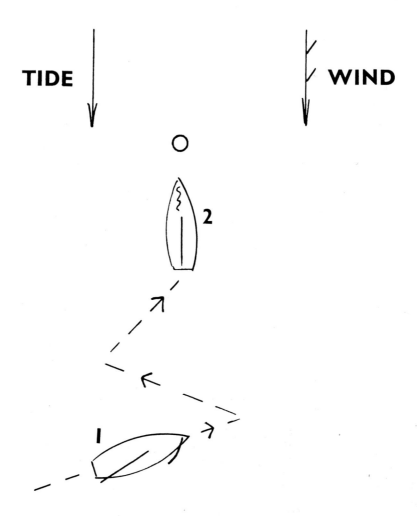

Fig. 2.7   Tacking up to a buoy with wind and tide together

out in a reasonably calm manner without undue flurry. It is interesting to watch the experienced skipper in these circumstances. Almost invariably his approach run up to the buoy is carried out more slowly than the same manoeuvre tackled by the inexperienced man. Remember therefore to proceed as calmly and as slowly as you can, whilst keeping sufficient way on the vessel so as to be in full command of the situation.

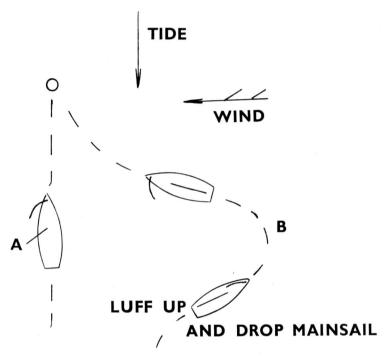

Fig. 2.8   Tacking up to a buoy with wind abeam

Choice of sails
Secondly, choice of sails. Most modern cruising yachts will handle under either the main or the foresail, even tacking to windward, although if working to windward under foresail alone, it is important to remember when tacking that the vessel pays off well to leeward before picking up on the next tack. The object of the exercise, however, is to arrive over the buoy with minimum sail set, such that it can easily be furled as soon as the buoy is secured. If conditions permit it and there is a choice between using main or foresail, it is usually preferable to use the mainsail and thus leave the foredeck clear for securing to the buoy. It is essential,however, to ensure that the mainsheet is freed as soon as possible to obviate any possibility of the sail taking charge whilst securing to the buoy. If it is decided that the approach run will be under foresail it will be necessary for the vessel to be rounded up some distance from the buoy to drop and secure the

main. It is essential that this is carried out in a smart and seamanlike manner. The topping lift should be hauled sufficiently to take up the weight of the boom in advance of the operation. As the vessel is rounded up, the main halyard should be released at the moment the vessel is pointing directly into the wind. The mainsail can then be easily dropped and roughly furled and secured with ties or better still with the shock cord loops mentioned earlier. These consist of short lengths of shock cord sufficiently long to pass round the roughly furled sail, with an eye in one end and a nylon hook on the other. Having rapidly secured the mainsail and hauled in on the mainsheet the vessel can then bear away under foresail and proceed to pick up the buoy.

The escape route

The final point that is worth remembering is the "escape route". When coming up to a mooring under sail in difficult conditions there is always the possibility of missing the mooring due to unforeseen circumstances, such as a sudden squall for example, and it is as well to have a fairly clear idea of an alternative plan of action. This is particularly important if the moorings are close together as is normally the case nowadays. The success of all operations involving "ship handling" depend on a sound knowledge of how one's vessel will behave in any given set of circumstances. No opportunity should be missed to ascertain how the vessel behaves under power and under sail. The information, once gained, can prove invaluable when manoeuvring in confined spaces.

LEAVING MOORINGS

It is not proposed to discuss the drill for leaving moorings under auxiliary power, as this should not present any difficulty. To carry out the operation under sail can be more difficult and warrants some thought. The direction of the wind must be carefully considered, for example if the wind is blowing from astern it would be difficult to set the mainsail as it would immediately fill and take charge and it would not be possible to spill the wind from it. In these circumstances the foresail should be set first with sheets free, the buoy rope cast off, foresail sheets hauled slightly and the vessel can then move into a suitable position for rounding up and setting the mainsail.

If the vessel is pointing into the wind, either main or foresail or both can be set and the vessel can then pay off on the most convenient tack. With wind abeam or abaft the beam the foresail would normally be the only sail set until the vessel has cleared the mooring and can round up into the wind to set the mainsail.

BERTHING ALONGSIDE—HANDLING UNDER POWER

In considering the problems of berthing alongside, that is, against a harbour wall or in a marina, the assumption is made that the auxiliary engine is used. In general, unless circumstances are unusually favourable, to attempt to berth under sail is an unnecessarily risky operation and, would not be attemped by the prudent seaman. If circumstances are such that the auxiliary is not available, a line should be put ashore at the earliest opportunity and the vessel warped into position. Before examining the problem associated with the actual berthing operation it is as well to have a clear idea of the way the particular yacht will handle under power.

The auxiliary vessel under power

At the risk of repeating some of the statements in Power Boat Handling, it is felt that too much emphasis cannot be placed on taking every opportunity to find out how the vessel behaves under power. Unlike the motor yacht, the sailing vessel designed primarily for propulsion by means of forces acting above the waterline, on occasions is not so certain in her movements under power, particularly when going astern. In a sailing vessel with an auxiliary engine it is important to realise that the propeller has side thrust as well as ahead or astern thrust. Most auxiliary yachts have a right-handed propeller and this gives a positive force at right angles to the fore and aft line which tends to move the stern to starboard when going ahead (the reason for this as explained elsewhere is that the lower half of the propeller, being in deeper and therefore denser water than the top half, exerts a greater force to the right than the corresponding thrust to the left of the top half of the propeller). Naturally, when going astern with a right-handed propeller, the stern tends to kick to port.

Making a tight turn

Knowledge of these characteristics can be very useful when a vessel is being manoeuvred

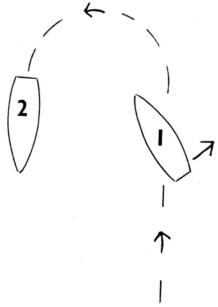

*Fig. 2.9 Tight turn right handed prop
kicking stern to starboard*

in a confined space. For example, if the stern kicks to starboard when going ahead, it follows that a much tighter turn can be made by turning to port, see Fig. 2.9. It will be

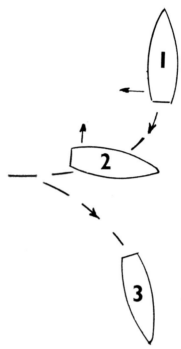

Fig. 2.10   *Tight reverse turn utilizing stern thrust to port (right handed prop)*

obvious that a turn to starboard will be very much wider as the natural movement of the propeller is acting against the force of the rudder. If it was necessary to turn the vessel round short in a tight turn and it was difficult to do this on a port hand turn, the reverse technique can be utilised. For example, a stiff breeze blowing from the port side might exert more pressure for'ard where the windage is generally greater, thus blowing the bows off to starboard. To attempt a tight turn to port in these circumstances would be difficult and might have unforeseen results. If, however, the vessel is given a kick astern on the auxiliary, this will thrust the stern to port and, coupled with the starboard thrust of the wind on the bows will enable a tight stern first move to be made, see Fig. 2.10. The combination of these two movements can form the basis of most tight manoeuvres and is particularly useful when berthing alongside in a harbour or marina. The main point to remember is to give a good burst on the throttle. If the latter is opened up gently the vessel will begin to move astern or ahead before the side thrust takes effect. Remember also that in general there is more effective power available when going ahead than astern in the normal auxiliary yacht. Summarising— when manoeuvring an auxiliary yacht in confined spaces, use short bursts of full throttle, this combined with full helm, makes the most effective use of the forces available.

Coming alongside

Prior to coming alongside, the vessel should be properly prepared for the manoeuvre; head and stern ropes should be available in their proper position, together with at least one spare line, all suitably coiled and ready for passing ashore. If the mooring lines are fairly heavy a light heaving line with a "monkey's paw" on the end may come in useful. Adequate fenders, both in size and number should be secured on that side of the vessel which will lie alongside the quay. A boat hook should be available up for'ard, if moving into a dock a second boat hook aft can be extremely useful on occasions.

The main influence when berthing is the wind. In general, the tidal stream in marinas or alongside quays in harbours, is usually slight although, of course, there are exceptions to this.

Assuming that the wind is blowing along the jetty, as shown in Fig. 2.11, the general approach would be to move in head to wind. As soon as the vessel is alongside, the head rope should be passed ashore and secured as far ahead as possible and not close,

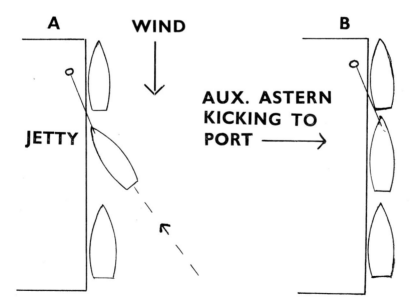

Fig. 2.11   Coming alongside

alongside the stem head. A short burst astern will not only stop the vessel but help to swing her stern into the quayside. The stern rope should then be run out and secured, immediately after which the fenders should be checked for position to ensure that the yacht's topsides are not in contact with any piles, etc. After this the final mooring operation is to secure the fore and aft springs and, if considered necessary, the breast ropes. It is difficult to consider all the many combinations of circumstances that may arise in berthing alongside and, indeed, unnecessary. A prudent skipper will prefer to work out his own approach to each problem when he is fully aware of the reaction of his ship to helm and propeller under all circumstances.

Use of springs, breast ropes, etc.

To be properly moored alongside a quay, a vessel requires to be secured with bow and stern ropes, breast ropes and springs, as shown in Figure 2.12. The bow and stern ropes have an obvious function to fulfil whilst the springs are equally important in that they prevent the vessel surging in a fore and aft direction under the influence of tidal streams or currents caused by ship movements in the vicinity. The breast ropes ensure that the vessel is kept close in to the quay, thereby ensuring that it can be boarded without undue risk. Referring back to the springs, the adjustment of these is particularly

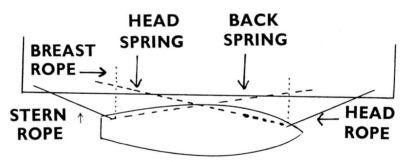

Fig. 2.12   Vessel moored alongside quay

important where there is any possibility of tidal streams. Correctly adjusted the springs will ensure that the vessel rides quietly, parallel with the side of the quay—if it should be necessary at any time to make fast alongside an anchored vessel the provision of the springs is vital and, suitably adjusted will permit the two vessels to ride slightly apart from each other, thereby reducing wear and tear on fenders.

Leaving the quayside

The most difficult situations usually occur with an onshore wind when the vessel has to leave the quayside and other vessels are moored immediately ahead and astern. In these circumstances it may be necessary to spring off or take a line out to some convenient pile or dockside, thus enabling the vessel to be warped head to wind and then moved out under power. If no other point is available it may be necessary to lay out a kedge and thus warp the vessel round, see Fig. 2.13.

Springing off is a technique whereby the head or stern of a vessel can be given a sheer away from the jetty when moving off. The operation is very simple and effective when carried out in a smart and seamanlike manner. Assuming that it is desired to turn the vessel's head away from the jetty, the procedure is as follows. Cast off breast, head and stern ropes and having ensured that the auxiliary is ready, cast off the head spring and give a touch astern with the auxiliary. The vessel will not be able to move astern due to the tension of the back spring but the combined effect of the propeller thrust and the spring will be to move the quarter into the jetty and consequently point the head out from the jetty, see Fig. 2.14. As soon as there is a clear way ahead the spring should be smartly slipped and the auxiliary put ahead. Particular care must be taken to ensure that there are adequate fenders correctly positioned on the quarter before the manoeuvre is attempted, as considerable strain can be placed on this pivoting point. The reverse

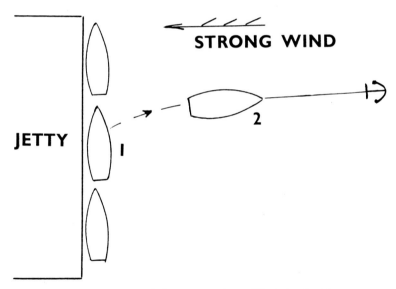

Fig. 2.13 *Using kedge to move from difficult berth with strong onshore wind*

procedure can be adopted if it is more expedient to attempt to move from the jetty stern first. In this case the head spring is used and the auxiliary put ahead, thus using the bow as the pivoting point and then moving astern as soon as the quarter is clear of the vessel astern.

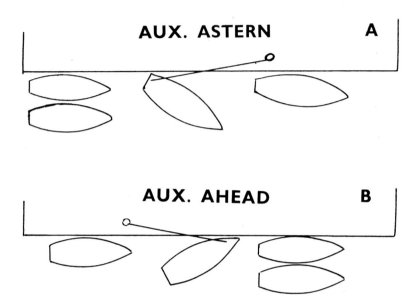

Fig. 2.14   Springing off

SECURING IN BERTHS THAT DRY OUT

At the risk of stating the obvious, it is rather important before lying alongside to ensure that any drying out berth has a suitable bottom with no obstructions and, equally important that the side of the jetty is suitable for lying against.

Assuming that the vessel is moored in the selected berth, the head rope, stern rope and springs should be suitably adjusted to allow for fall of tide, it may, of course, be necessary to repeat this operation at intervals until the vessel has settled. Naturally, the longer the ropes are when first set up, the fewer adjustments will be required between high water and low water. The siting and adjustment of the fenders is particularly important when they are required to remain effective throughout the fall of the tide. It will be unusual for a quayside to be smooth and present no particular problems as the vessel drops down on the tide. If, for example, a quay is faced with wooden piles, it is difficult if not impossible to keep fenders in the correct position, that is between the vessel's top sides and the pile face, see Fig. 2.15. One method of overcoming this difficulty is to secure a plank or spar of suitable length outside the fenders but attached to the vessel's side. This will then ride up and down comfortably on the piles, at the same time the top sides are adequately protected by the fenders. Having ensured that the vessel is properly secured, the next step is to ensure that at low water the vessel will be leaning in to the quay at a safe angle and unlikely to fall outwards. This is effected by giving the vessel a slight angle of heel while she is still afloat by placing some heavy weights, for example the main anchor and cable, on the deck adjacent to the quayside or similarly altering the heel of the vessel, see Fig. 2.16. Alternatively, a halyard can be taken out from the masthead as shown in Fig. 2.16, suitably adjusted and with a weight in the bight. This must, of course, be sufficiently heavy to give a

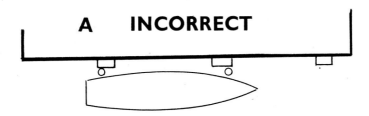

(a) incorrect—vessel may surge and fenders become ineffective.

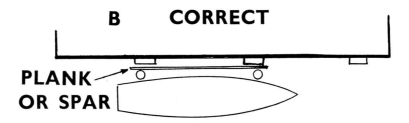

(b) correct—if vessel moves fore and aft fenders are still effective.

Fig. 2.15 Lying alongside quay with protruding obstructions—head and stern moorings and springs as usual.

reasonable angle of heel. This angle of heel depends to a certain extent on the particular circumstances of the situation but, in general, would be up to five degrees. Care must, however, be taken to see that the angle of heel is such that when grounded the mast and rigging will not foul the quay.

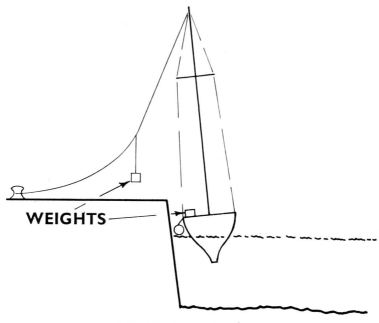

WEIGHTS

Fig. 2.16   Mooring in a drying out berth.

Note: Head and stern ropes may require tending as vessel drops down.
Similarly main halyard will also require adjustment.

BENDING, SETTING AND TAKING IN SAIL

There is probably little that one can say about setting sail that is not already known to the average cruising man. The mechanics of setting the foresail, hauling up the mainsail, should be so well known that it is not proposed to deal with them in detail here. It could be emphasised perhaps that the prudent owner will practice sail drill in the dark— spreader lights have been known to fail. It will be noted that the roping on a sail is always on the port side, knowledge of this fact will avoid the embarrassment of hoisting a foresail upside down. On the other hand, it is not unusual to see a fast modern design of cruiser behaving indifferently because of sails incorrectly set and a few words on this subject may not therefore be out of place. In the modern offshore cruiser/racer the almost universal rig of Bermudian sloop has been refined down to the point of extreme simplicity. The only real complication in the rig comes when the handling of a spinnaker is considered. The effective setting and handling of this sail requires more skill and experience than the setting of the normal fore and aft sail. This is, however, rather outside the scope of this chapter which is concerned basically with the principles of ship handling, particularly in harbour.

The set of the sails

The golden rule in connection with sail setting is that the luff is set up as hard as the gear will permit. Reference to any of the standard works on sail design and efficiency will show that a straight leading edge in the aerofoil section is extremely important. A slack luff, whether it be in foresail or mainsail, will reduce the efficiency of the sail by a surprising extent. Apart from reducing the speed of the vessel it will also increase the leeway angle, that is, the course made good off the wind. The net result of a drop in speed and less ground made good to windward can prove very depressing to an inexperienced owner who may assume that the fault lies with the yacht designer, instead of realising that he can transform his boat's performance with a few simple adjustments of sheets and halyards. In similar manner it is essential that the leech of the sail also presents a smooth edge to the air flow which is leaving the sail at that particular point. The functions of the battens in the leech of a mainsail are well known in that they flatten the leech thereby preventing any obstruction to the air flow which would reduce the speed of the vessel. Provision is made in some mainsails for a further adjustment of the leech by means of the use of a small leechline running down inside the seam of the leech. This is provided to vary the tension in the leech according to the force of the wind.

Likewise, it is especially important to see that the leech of the foresail and/or Genoa are equally well adjusted and not in any way curling at the leech and thereby obstructing the air flow across the sail. This curl or hook in the leech of a foresail is usually produced by an incorrect sheeting point, the usual trouble being that the point is too far forward. The selection of the sheeting point is extremely important and in the average offshore cruising yacht, track slides are provided, enabling the foresail sheet blocks to be readily moved fore and aft, depending on the size of the sail that is set.

Chapter Three

Sailing Yachts—
Handling and Safety at Sea

PREPARING FOR SEA

Safety at sea depends primarily on preparation. Preparation of the vessel and gear, adequate consideration of the navigational problems that may occur on the trip and last but not least, personal preparation by the skipper. By this is meant that knowledge of shiphandling that can take years to acquire, but, with application, can rapidly become second nature. It is most important to acquire the habit of critically examining every manoeuvre carried out with the vessel to determine whether or not it could have been improved. By analysing the way the vessel handles under various conditions the observant owner will rapidly acquire a knowledge of his vessel that will enable him to handle it with understanding in difficult situations. The greatest test of all—that of safely surviving a gale or near gale at sea is one which may perhaps never occur. It is therefore particularly important to prepare oneself for a situation such as this by at least considering the problems that will arise and some of the lines of action required to deal with them. Clear thinking when cold, wet and possibly exhausted is difficult; some pre-conceived ideas may be very useful.

This then is the essence of personal preparation—to have clear ideas on possible courses of action in the difficult situations that may arise.

CHECKING OVER THE VESSEL AND GEAR

It is assumed that during the annual fitting out a thorough check of hull, spars, running and standing rigging has been carried out and the sails have been returned to the sailmaker for the inevitable repairs that are necessary.

During the course of a normal cruising season with perhaps one or two trips to foreign parts it is surprising how much wear can take place. The prudent seaman will therefore make a habit of checking over his vessel prior to any trip that takes him offshore—in this context meaning out of sight of land—a situation where in the event of trouble he is entirely dependent on his own resources. In the case of a well found ship this check would be a simple one consisting of an examination along the following lines:

(1) Standing rigging—a quick visual check for impending trouble, not forgetting that binoculars can be useful when looking aloft.

(2) Running rigging—check places where undue chafe or wear may have taken place, examine any shackles that are not permanently moused.

(3) Reefing gear—check gearing if roller reefing—if point reefing, are pendants ready and located in their proper stowage?

(4) Sails—these should normally receive a quick examination when being handled. In these days of tough terylene materials damage to the sail itself is infrequent, the biggest chance of trouble lies with the stitching. Unlike the softer cotton sails the stitching tends to remain proud on terylene sails and is therefore liable to chafe.

(5) The hull—the most important check here is the bilge pumps. Are they working properly—are the strum boxes clean and are the bilges free of extraneous material in the form of old rag, etc., which might clog the system at a critical moment? With the modern type of diaphragm pump this possibility has decreased, but still exists. Are the cockpit drains clean and free? The practice of pouring a bucket of water down daily if none has come aboard is worth considering.

(6) Equipment—under this heading comes the important items of safety equipment— distress rockets, flares, hand torches (are the batteries okay?), personal buoyancy (enough for everyone who will be on board), safety harnesses for everyone, not only for those who will be working on deck.

(7) Navigational equipment—charts to cover the course and those other places that one may be driven to by stress of weather—Admiralty pocket tidal stream atlas— Reed's Almanac, etc.

The various items mentioned above can form the basis of a check list which the owner can build up for himself and quickly run over at regular intervals during the season, thereby ensuring that his vessel is always in a seamanlike state.

MANAGEMENT OF SMALL VESSELS IN HEAVY WEATHER

Considering the large number of small yachts around our coasts the percentage of those that become involved in really heavy weather is remarkably small. The average cruising man appreciates that it does not take a force eight gale to stress both himself and his ship. It is said that a yachtsman's gale is really only force six and, it is undoubtedly true that sailing can become uncomfortable and difficult for the family cruiser of modest dimensions in anything exceeding force five. Bearing in mind that really heavy weather, as opposed to unpleasant conditions, does not often occur in the average cruising man's life it is most important to be at least theoretically familiar with the conditions that may arise and the possible methods of countering them.

Early warning

The prudent yachtsman on passage will normally listen to the weather forecasts for the region in which he is sailing in order to obtain maximum advance warning of any heavy weather. In addition he will watch the weather portents in order to ascertain the local situation, knowing that weather forecasts of necessity cover a large sea area and local conditions may vary from that to be expected from a necessarily broad picture.

Preparations for heavy weather—food

Below decks all gear should be properly stowed and lashed down and preparations made to have food and drink available during the passage if it is anticipated that cooking in the galley may become too difficult. The presence on board of one or two large thermos flasks to contain hot water for preparing coffee or Bovril during the blow can be very useful. Boiling water in the galley of a small cruiser during a blow is difficult and potentially dangerous and worth avoiding if possible.

Prepare some food that will be easily eaten in difficult circumstances, here again if one of the larger thermos flasks is filled with hot soup the effect on the morale of the crew when it is served later will be out of all proportion to the effort involved in preparing it.

On deck

On deck the hatches should be well secured, canvas covers fitted if available and all openings closed as far as is possible—for example the anchor chain hawse pipe should be stuffed with rag to prevent any water finding its way below.

All gear carried on deck must be well lashed down, particularly anything of a heavy nature such as a dinghy. Life lines must be rigged in such positions that any crew member can leave the cockpit and go forward to the foredeck without having to unclip his safety harness. All crew members on deck must wear personal buoyancy in addition to their safety harnesses.

Course of action

The prudent seaman will weigh up the situation, bearing in mind his present position, the probable course and speed of the storm and its resultant effects on wind speed and direction, the position of any possible ports of refuge and, of course, the characteristics of the craft concerned. The main alternatives that will face him are:

(*a*) maintain present course.
(*b*) stand out to obtain a good offing from the coast.
(*c*) run for shelter.

THE ARRIVAL OF BAD WEATHER

Running

Every yachtsman will be familiar with the apparent wind increase when altering course from a run to a beat and this exemplifies one of the dangers to watch for when on passage. When running it is easy to fall into the trap of carrying on too long when conditions are deteriorating. In the first place it may not be obvious that the vessel is becoming over pressed until there is perhaps an involuntary gybe and secondly there is always a tendency to put off an unpleasant job in the hope that conditions may improve. The longer reefing is deferred the more difficult and indeed dangerous the task becomes.

Beating to windward

If the course is close hauled or beating to windward there is usually little difficulty in determining when to reef. There is no doubt about the strength of the wind and condi-

tions generally usually become very unpleasant before they become dangerous.
On this point of sailing reefing is a comparatively simple operation as the vessel is readily "hove to" without the necessity of rounding up in a "smooth".

Reefing

Consider first the situation in which the vessel is running before the wind and the decision to reef has been taken.

No matter how confused the sea appears close observation will indicate that at intervals "smooths" occur when the sea is less irregular. A careful watch should be maintained and the vessel rounded up to windward at a suitable opportunity when there is a minimum chance of catching a sea broadside on.

Dependent on the actual point of sailing, it is usually possible to change the foresail whilst still running. If this is difficult it can be left until the vessel has rounded up and is pointing into the wind. If the vessel is fitted with twin forestays the replacement foresail can be hanked on prior to the actual changeover thereby facilitating the operation.

It is worth remembering that even with a single forestay it is not necessary to remove one foresail before setting the replacement. It can be hanked on to the forestay between the lower hank and foot of the sail that is already set, when this is dropped it is only necessary to unclip the hanks on it, transfer the halliard to the new sail and set it.

When reefing the main, the weight of the boom should first be taken on the topping lift, then the main halliard lowered away whilst winding the boom (assuming roller reefing). One of the disadvantages of roller reefing gear is the tendency for the after end of the boom to drop when several rolls have been wound in the sail. This occurs due to the build up of the luff rope at the inboard end of the boom effectively increasing its diameter at that point. It can be overcome by fitting a batten at the outboard end which has the effect of increasing the boom diameter and thereby compensating for the build up of the luff rope at the other end. If, however, this is not sufficiently effective it is important to take some steps to ensure that the boom end does not endanger anyone in the cockpit. One rough and ready method would be to roll in an empty sail bag or similar article that will not damage the sail but will at the same time effectively increase the boom diameter. At least one sail maker is now using a luff tape instead of a rope as a means of overcoming the problem.

Heaving to

Heaving to consists essentially of luffing up, backing the foresail to weather and lashing the helm slightly a 'lee. No doubt the operation will have been tried out on many occasions before it is necessary to resort to it in hard weather. The actual position of the helm and trim of the sails will, however, require some adjusting until the point is found where the vessel is riding comfortably and safely. When this has been settled the skipper should note the speed and course made good under these conditions in order that he can maintain his D.R. plot.

D.R. position and plot

It is assumed that the D.R. position has been worked up to the position where the vessel has hove to. The navigator will now require to know the speed at which the vessel is forereaching and the course made good. This established he will then consider the amount of sea room available to leeward and the probable duration of the blow. For example, the weather forecast indicates that the blow will last for say 10 hours, the vessel is forereaching at two knots at 90° to the wind and probable surface drift is two knots. The sea room required to leeward would be approx. 18 miles for reasonable safety. This calculation excludes the effect of tidal currents which must, of course, be included. Having considered all these aspects the skipper then has to make the decision whether to continue hove to, knowing that he has adequate sea room to leeward or, if this is not the case, to resume sailing to make a good offing before heaving to becomes essential.

Working up to windward

Assuming that there is insufficient sea room and it is necessary to work upwind as long as possible it is essential to sail "full and by" to maintain sufficient speed to drive over the heavy seas.

The temptation will be to reef right down to the point where the vessel is more comfortable but making little ground to windward. The modern small light displacement cruiser has to be driven hard to maintain good progress. In particular the popular family twin bilge keeler will not perform as well as the single deep keel vessel of similar water line. The performance of the latter, when designed for fast off shore work can be quite surprising provided the crew is tough enough to take it. Driving to windward in these conditions demands an experienced helmsman if the best is to be obtained from the vessel. He will feel how far to luff up to a breaking crest, being careful not to luff too far, immediately bearing away to pick up speed to drive over the next crest.

The deteriorating situation

The important points to remember, which are frequently mentioned in all accounts of hard weather sailing is that the well found ship will take more punishment than the crew, and secondly that the deeper the water the safer the situation.

If it is not possible to make harbour while conditions can be considered safe for the vessel concerned then every effort must be made to establish a good offing as soon as possible. In general this decision may not be too difficult to make as if there is not time to make harbour then the vessel will probably be sufficiently off shore to maintain a good offing provided, of course, we are considering an average summer "blow" of comparatively short duration.

Assuming that the vessel has been hove to and the weather is deteriorating to the point where it is dangerous to keep any sail up at all the skipper is faced with the alternatives of lying to a sea anchor, running under bare pole with warps streamed astern or lying a 'hull. The choice depends on many factors, but the important ones are the sea room available and the wave characteristics, apart of course, from the obvious one of the characteristics of the particular vessel concerned. Considering first the characteristics of the sea—the short steep seas found in the Southern North Sea can be troublesome if the vessel lies beam on or is liable to broach to. The danger here is the possibility of the vessel being rolled over on the crest of a wave and receiving a severe knock down blow which may cause considerable damage to the large ports, or rather windows, fitted in the average off shore cruiser.

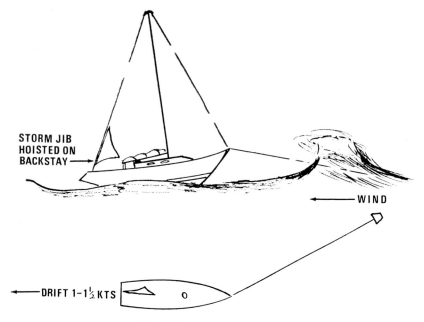

STORM JIB
HOISTED ON
BACKSTAY

WIND

DRIFT 1–1½ KTS

Fig. 3.1 Lying to a Sea Anchor

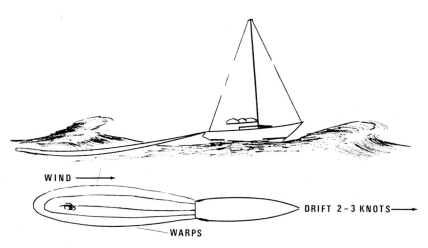

WIND

DRIFT 2–3 KNOTS

WARPS

Fig 3.2 Running with Warps Streamed

Lying a 'hull

With all sail stripped off the vessel is allowed to take up her own natural position. The modern easily driven hull will tend to drive ahead due to the wind pressure on the mast, this can be corrected by lashing the helm slightly a 'lee to make her luff up if she fore reaches at any appreciable speed.

The small light displacement cruiser should ride out a hard blow in safety in this manner, rather as a cork in that no resistance is offered to breaking crests, the only real danger being that of having a port hole smashed in.

Running with warps streamed

Sea room permitting it may be easier and perhaps safer to run under bare pole downwind with sufficient warps streamed astern to form a drag. In this situation it is, of course, necessary to be able to stream sufficient warps to form an appreciable drag in order to keep the vessel stern on to the following sea and thereby reducing the risk of broaching to. This method has the disadvantage that the stern of the vessel, the weaker part, is presented to the following seas. In a full gale the possibility will exist of a following wave crest lifting the stern and damaging the rudder. In general, however, the consensus of opinion of experienced seamen is that this is one of the safest methods of riding out a gale.

Lying to a sea anchor

This is the classical method of riding out a storm familiar to all students of marine literature. It has the merit of being a well tried and proven method for shallow draft craft but does, of course, depend on a well made sea anchor as the strains involved will obviously be considerable. The small, very light displacement craft can lie satisfactorily to a sea anchor under bare pole, but the heavier displacement vessel may require a steadying sail aft to keep her pointing head to wind in the stronger gusts. Whilst this can be achieved quite easily in the yawl the only satisfactory solution in the case of a sloop is to set a small storm jib on the back stay. If this is done it will be necessary to provide a halliard which is probably best effected by lashing the boom down and using the topping lift. One of the advantages of the sea anchor is that less leeway is made and this in itself can be extremely useful in the confined waters of the Strait of Dover and the Southern North Sea.

Summarising—heavy weather drill

(1) Always take action in good time.

(2) Roll in too many turns rather than too few—it's easy to shake them out.

(3) Remember to keep a careful watch when running and do not let the vessel become over pressed.

(4) Having reefed watch the weather situation carefully and reduce to bare pole or sea anchor in good time.

(5) Keep a D.R. plot going and do not forget that surface drift may increase leeway by as much as two knots.

(6) Keep a look out on deck and at night ensure that a powerful light is available and white Very flares.

(7) At night in heavy weather the average yacht's navigation lights are hardly effective, a powerful masthead light under these conditions whilst not complying with the Collision Regulations will at least indicate to the big ship man that *something* is there.

(8) A radar reflector, particularly at night can be of immense help in indicating the vessel's position to all interested parties. Under no circumstances should a yacht proceed to sea without one.

(9) Finally, the most important item of equipment—the crew. Every effort should be made to produce hot drinks and some form of food to delay the onset of exhaustion. Any member not actively engaged on deck should be getting as much rest below as possible—preferably warmly wrapped up in his bunk.

NAVIGATING IN FOG

When fog is expected
When navigating in conditions when fog can reasonably be anticipated it is particularly important to correct the estimated position on the chart at frequent intervals. The sudden onset of fog banks produces a difficult and worrying situation which is partially alleviated if the navigator knows precisely what his position is at that moment. It is essential to maintain the D.R. plot thereafter as accurately as possible. If it is not already hoisted, the radar reflector should be sent aloft immediately.

Course to steer—coastwise
In normal weather the natural instinct of the sailing man is to keep in deep water but in fog the situation requires a rather different outlook. The navigator's first reaction must be to leave the deep water shipping lanes, if possible for the comparative safety of the shallows and sandbanks. It is worth remembering that the meteorological conditions that produce fog in general also produce only moderate winds and the dangers associated with shallow waters are thereby reduced. Having taken the decision to alter course regular checks must then be made on the echo sounder (or hand lead if no echo sounder is fitted) until the vessel is in soundings and clear of the shipping lanes. If the vessel is fitted with R.D.F. this will be an extremely useful aid to the navigator when used in conjunction with his echo sounder and patent log. It should be borne in mind, however, when closing the coast line that a D.F. bearing tends to become unreliable as the bearing becomes parallel to the coast. (For further information on this point see Reed's Coastal Navigation in this Series). Regard must be paid to the necessary sound signals to be made by vessels under way in fog or restricted visibility. (See chapter on the—Collision Regulations page 67). In the case of a motor cruiser the provision of

an adequate fog horn presents no difficulties but this is not necessarily so in the case of the sailing yacht which may not have an adequate battery. The regulations do not require the use of a fog horn in any vessel under 40 feet in length but it is obviously prudent to be able to make effective signals in difficult situations. In this connection the small cruiser should carry on board one of the aerosol operated fog horns which can deliver a remarkably powerful sound signal considering the size of the apparatus. Whilst this type of equipment has limitations in that the capacity of the container would not permit standard signals to be given for any length of time, it can be extremely useful when it is obvious that another vessel is in the near vicinity. A spare container should of course be kept on board.

Arrival in soundings

Having arrived in soundings the decision next required is whether to anchor until the fog clears or whether to proceed on a line of soundings, i.e. contour, in the required direction. The decision must be influenced by many factors and the prudent yachtsman will consider the situation very carefully before deciding to proceed, rather than anchor and wait for the fog to lift. If the D.R. position is known to be reasonably accurate and the coastal configuration is suitable then further progress can be made by running along a depth contour, assuming that this offers a safe course and does not pass close to any obvious dangers such as wrecks or headlands where the shore may become steep to. Every effort should be made to check the vessel's position whenever possible by D.F. fixes etc.

Reaching the destination

When the desired destination is eventually reached the decision whether to enter or not depends primarily on its character. If it is a small port, or anchorage used entirely by yachts and perhaps fishermen, the careful seaman may well feel his way in, in safety. If, however, it is a busy commercial port an entry should not be attempted unless conditions are such that it is clearly safe to do so. Commercial traffic, operating with sophisticated electronic aids may be moving with safety but will be quite unable to avoid small craft which may get in their way.

Summarising

(1) Whenever fog is expected maintain an estimated position as accurately as possible.

(2) Ensure that the radar reflector is hoisted.

(3) If outward bound try to get as far as possible from the main shipping lanes.

(4) If inward bound get in to soundings as soon as possible.

(5) Do not attempt to enter any harbour unless it is clearly safe to do so.

(6) Maintain a lookout as good as possible in the circumstances.

(7) Have the best possible fog signal available for use on board.

WEATHER FORECASTS

B.B.C.

A knowledge of the basic weather situations as it is likely to affect him is one of the most important things that the cruising man should know. It is not good practice to ignore the barometer and weather forecasts when conditions look good. The good seaman will pay as much attention to them when the sun is shining as he will when there are obvious storm clouds to windward. In this way he is building up all the time a mental picture of the changing weather situation and is far less likely to be taken by surprise than the man who listens in occasionally. The B.B.C. shipping forecasts provide an excellent overall picture for European coastal waters and now that the 1755 hours forecast has been lengthened to five minutes and the 0200 hours one moved back to 0030 there is now a good general forecast available at 6 hourly intervals throughout the 24 hours.

Coastal stations

Using these forecasts as a basis and tuning to the coastal radio stations on the trawler wave band (1·5—3·5kHz.), together with foreign weather broadcasts in English, it is possible to obtain weather information at very frequent intervals.

For example, on a fairly short passage of approx. 90 miles, from Burnham to Ostend, it is possible to obtain weather information at almost two hourly intervals by listening in turn to the B.B.C. Shipping forecasts, North Foreland, Ostend Radio and Scheveningen Radio.

It is true, of course, that the coastal stations both British and foreign are concerned with a smaller area than the B.B.C. Shipping forecast and are for that reason more useful when in or approaching those areas.

It is a good plan when cruising in any particular area to make out a sheet giving details of the stations that can be received in that area on a time basis. All these stations are listed with full details in Reed's Nautical Almanac but are naturally enough shown in areas. It is suggested that stations should be selected and listed in time order throughout the day so that a forecast can be picked up whenever one is available throughout the day without unnecessary research into the Almanac.

For example, considering the passage from Burnham to Ostend—a weather forecast sheet could be made up on the following lines:

Time B.S.T.	Station	Frequency
0030	B.B.C.	200kHz.
0330	Scheveningen	420kHz.
0630	B.B.C.	200kHz.
0903	North Foreland	1848kHz.
0920	Ostend	435kHz.
0930	Scheveningen	420kHz.
*1355	B.B.C.	200kHz.
1530	Scheveningen	420kHz.

and so on.

*Monday to Saturday only, but 1155 on Sunday

It is not suggested that the skipper will necessarily listen to all these broadcasts but with this information readily available he is able to see at a glance when the next forecast is due should he need one.

Recording the information

It is easy for the novice to assume that he can remember the part of a forecast which is of interest to him. It is, however, remarkably easy to forget details unless they are recorded immediately and for this reason alone the navigator is strongly recommended to note the information as broadcast on one of the specially prepared forms, which can be readily obtained, showing the areas. In this way there is no danger of forgetting vital facts and in addition the overall weather picture is built up.

It is convenient when using these charts to use the standard notations for indicating wind strength and direction. In this way the information can be taken down rapidly and accurately and thus provides an immediate picture of the wind situation which is far more readily assimilated than a written list of wind speeds and directions.

Land area regional forecasts

One factor not always fully appreciated by yachtsmen is that the shipping forecast is for "the next 24 hours" and does not mention any possibilities beyond that period. The land weather forecasts usually include a "further outlook" which extends two days beyond this period and on occasions may give him a lead that will help him to avoid trouble if he is on a long passage.

The land forecasts should therefore form a "must" for every yachtsman who wishes to be well informed on the subject of the weather.

Summarising, the prudent mariner will always:

(1) Obtain a weather forecast before setting off on passage.

(2) Listen to the main shipping forecasts without fail.

(3) Prepare a list of coastal stations available en route and listen as circumstances dictate.

(4) Record information obtained in order to maintain a "weather picture".

It need hardly be said that in addition to the above the yachtsman will watch his own barometer at regular intervals and also observe local meteorological conditions.

THE ANEROID BAROMETER

With the almost universal installation of some form of radio receiver in modern yachts there is a tendency to rely heavily on shipping forecasts from the B.B.C. and coastal stations. This is good practice in so far as the properly prepared forecast, based on information obtained from many sources, is necessarily superior to single observer forecasting based only on local conditions.

It should never be forgotten, however, that radio sets can fail and the yachtsman who is familiar with the methods of local prediction by observation is in a much safer position than the man who is thrown on his own resources without adequate preparation.

By courtesy of Henry Browne & Son Ltd.
Fig. 3.3 The Aneroid Barometer

To be able to forecast local weather for a few hours ahead is a valuable ability, and one that can be acquired by an individual who is prepared to work at the problem. The student will no doubt have carefully studied the companion volume to this book on Meteorology and it is not therefore proposed to deal in detail with either the Aneroid barometer or the principles of meteorology.

The point that must be emphasised, however, is the necessity to build up a real understanding of the subject, and to appreciate that barometer readings, properly interpreted are the biggest single factor in successfully forecasting local weather for a few hours ahead.

An experienced single observer, with only local barometer readings and observations, is unlikely to be able to forecast weather accurately for more than six to eight hours ahead at any given time; even this short period, however, can be very useful on occasions.

Brief summary of barometer indication

(1) The rapidity of the variation in pressure usually reflects both the speed of the approaching weather and its severity.

(2) Low pressure, i.e. below 1000 millibars shows unstable and changing conditions.

(3) High pressure, i.e. above say 1005 millibars shows stable and continuing fair conditions, although the yachtsman should remember that strong winds can still accompany high pressures although the winds may not reach gale force.

(4) In general the slower the variation the longer the particular weather is likely to last, a slow steady rise for example usually presages a reasonably lengthy period of good weather lasting several days at least.

(5) Rapid variations on the other hand indicate the speedy approach of unstable conditions. If it is a rapid fall the bad weather will arrive speedily whilst if it is a rapid rise it would be unwise to consider that fair weather is necessarily on the way. It may indeed indicate a worsening of conditions, i.e. weather may become more squally. It is important to know what is meant by a rapid rise or fall and in this context is unlikely to exceed 5 millibars in a period of three hours, in the Southern part of the British Isles and North Sea. In other areas, notably to the N.W. of the British Isles this rate of variation could be doubled for the same type of weather.

(6) In home waters a falling barometer is usually associated with Southerly gales and Northerly ones with a rising one.

Chapter Four

Power Boat Handling

If you can handle a sailing vessel, albeit only a dinghy, you will learn to handle a powered boat quickly. Remember that in a powered boat one can always GO ASTERN.

EFFECT OF PROPELLER

If a boat has a propeller, which viewed from astern, turns clockwise when the engine is put ahead, it is called a right handed propeller. See Fig. 4.1.

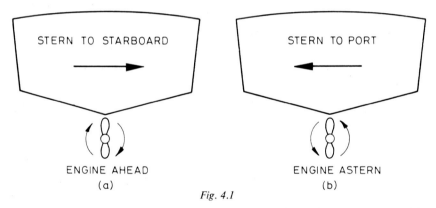

Fig. 4.1

When starting from rest, going ahead, the boat's bow will tend to go to port and her stern to starboard. This can be counteracted by the rudder. Once the boat has way upon her this effect is not so noticeable.

When going astern the stern will go to port quite sharply. The rudder will not counteract this until the boat has good sternway upon her when she may be steered, but with much less efficiency than when going ahead.

If the propeller is a left handed one, the above effects will be in the opposite direction. These effects are a combination of the transverse thrust, the screw race and the wake stream.

In Fig. 4.1(a) it will be seen that going ahead the upper blade moving to starboard, by pressing the water tries to push the stern to port, and the lower blade acts in the opposite direction. However, the lower blade being deeper, has greater effect and the stern moves to starboard.

It will be seen in Fig. 4.1(b) that going astern the lower blade, which again has the greater effect, is thrusting to starboard and thus the stern goes to port.

This effect is called the TRANSVERSE THRUST.

When stopping from going ahead the propeller usually has more effect if put to STOP, then SLOW ASTERN with a slow build up to Full Astern rather than putting it Full Astern immediately.

TURNING CIRCLES

This is the path of a ship when turning at steady speed under a steady helm. See Fig. 4.2.

The *Advance* is the distance ahead in the direction of the original course which the pivoting point travels after the tiller is put over.

The *Transfer* is the distance which the pivoting point travels in a direction at 90° to the original course.

The *Diameter* is that of the track when it becomes circular.

Notice that on putting the tiller over she will first move outwards bodily before beginning to turn. During the turn the stem will be inside the track of the pivoting point and the stern will be outside. After completing the turn she will be inside and ahead of her starting position.

If there is wind or tide effect her circle will be modified accordingly.

A fine lined speedy vessel will have a larger turning circle than a slow deep draughted one. Speed does not affect turning with deep draught to much extent but a shallow draught vessel's circle increases considerably as her speed rises.

WIND EFFECT

The extent of this depends upon the strength of the wind and the area available for pressure by the wind.

The way in which a ship reacts depends upon the position of her pivoting point.

Wind effect is more noticeable at low speeds. When stopped a ship tends to lie broadside on. When slowing down her bows tend to come up to, or fall off from, the wind depending upon its relative direction.

When going astern the pivoting point moves aft and the stern comes up into the wind causing the bows to fall off.

DRAUGHT AND TRIM

Handling is usually easiest when the trim is slightly by the stern. Stern trim increases the turning circle, bow trim decreases it.

SHALLOW WATER EFFECT

When in shallow water a ship tends to squat by the stern and her speed reduces due to the bigger bow and stern waves caused because the water she displaces cannot be replaced quickly between her bottom and the sea bed. She is liable to yaw and take longer to answer the rudder. Steering is also affected when moving slowly in shallows.

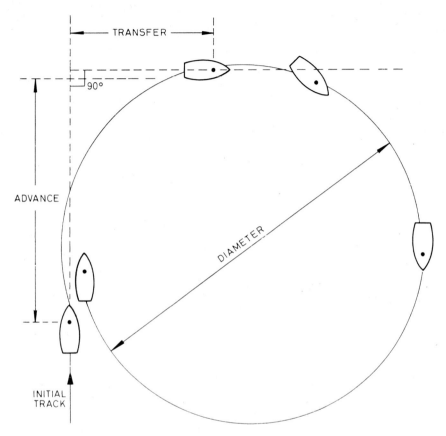

TRANSFER

90°

ADVANCE

DIAMETER

INITIAL
TRACK

Fig. 4.2   The Turning Circle

TURNING A BOAT SHORT ROUND—See Fig. 4.3

In a boat with a right handed propeller it is preferable to turn round to starboard as follows:

(*a*) Starboard your rudder, engine ahead. Do not run further or get more headway on than is consistent with the space you have in which to manoeuvre.

(*b*) Port your rudder, engine astern. As sternway is gathered the swing of the stern to port will be increased by rudder effect.

(*c*) Starboard your rudder, engine ahead.

(*d*) Rudder amidships, engine ahead.

In calm weather and no tidal stream or current you should be able to turn her round in this manner. When there is wind or stream effect or little room to turn you may find that you have to snub her round by dropping your anchor on the bottom at position "b" in Fig. 4.3. In this case you must only let out enough cable to allow the anchor to drag or dredge on the bottom as there is the danger, especially in a tideway, of breaking your cable. One school of thought says that this is the true way of turning short round. If the anchor is not used then all one is doing is to turn the boat round and the similarity to a three point turn in a motor car is very obvious.

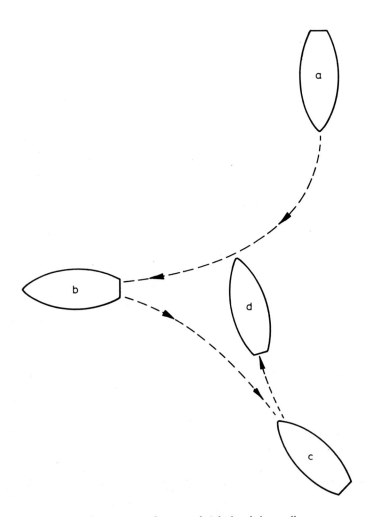

Fig. 4.3   Turning short round right handed propeller

MAKING FAST TO A BUOY

The boat should be headed for the buoy keeping it a little on the starboard bow so that when she comes astern to take the way off, the bow falling off to starboard has been allowed for. If there is some wind it is often better to approach the buoy with the wind astern and pass it to port. Now go astern on your engine so as to bring the wind on your starboard quarter and the buoy under the port bow. At this point go ahead on your engine to take off the sternway and as her stern swings into the wind the buoy may be picked up.

If you cannot approach the buoy in either of these ways because of tidal stream or obstructions, you should stop the boat to windward, with the bows abreast the buoy. As she drifts down on to the buoy pick it up and she will swing round head to wind.

ANCHORING

Choose a spot where you will have enough room to swing once she has brought up to the anchor. The amount of cable to veer varies but it should at least be enough to ensure that some is lying on the bottom where it leads away from the anchor. Any, other than a horizontal, pull on the anchor reduces its holding power. The more cable you veer out the less yawing or pitching you will get in the case of squalls or increase in the wind.

It is usual to let go the anchor when the vessel is stopped in the water but about to gather sternway. Let go a scope of cable equal to about twice the depth of water so that the anchor has a chance to grip. Allow her to come round to this and as the cable starts to grow ahead slack away until you have out sufficient to ride easily without snatching at the anchor.

If anchoring in a wind do it stopped and heading so that her stern will pay off in the desired direction. If anchoring in a tidal stream always stem it unless wind is present and stronger than the stream.

COMING ALONGSIDE AND SECURING

Do not do it at too great a speed. Normally only just maintain your steerage way. Remember, that when going astern the effect from the propeller will be to swing the bows to starboard and the stern to port, but that when close alongside the wash may build up pressure between the ship and the quay, if a solid one, and thus force the stern outwards.

Always stem the stream if any.

If going *port side alongside* approach at an angle of about 20° heading somewhat ahead of the berth but close enough to get a spring ashore. Go astern to bring her stern in and get a sternline ashore, at the same time passing a headline ashore.

If going *starboard side alongside* approach at a finer angle and heading for a point somewhat abaft of where the stem will be when she is secured. As her bows near the quay pass the headline ashore, put the rudder to port giving the engines a touch ahead. As she comes parallel with the berth go astern to take the way off then pass your sternline ashore.

Remember that if there is any wind you will have to make allowance for leeway during your run up to the berth and also for any slewing effect which will vary with different

vessels according to the amount and position of surface area each offers to the wind.
If the wind is blowing on to the berth it may be advisable to get a little ahead of but
broadside on to the berth and a little way off in order to drop your anchor. She may
then be given a sheer towards the berth by putting the helm up keeping her from
falling down heavily on the berth by checking on the cable. Once alongside and
secured the cable should be slacked right down. It will be a valuable aid for hauling off
if the wind is still blowing on departure.

To secure alongside your minimum moorings should consist of head and stern ropes
and forward and after springs. See Fig. 4.4.

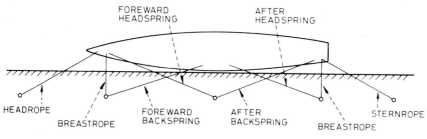

FOREWARD
HEADSPRING

AFTER
HEADSPRING

HEADROPE

BREASTROPE

FOREWARD
BACKSPRING

AFTER
BACKSPRING

BREASTROPE

STERNROPE

Fig. 4.4

Depending upon your length of stay and the weather any or all of these may be
doubled up.

The headrope, forward and after backsprings prevent the secured vessel from moving
aft. The sternrope, forward and after headsprings prevent the vessel from moving
forward. They each exert an athwartship pull tending to keep the vessel alongside.

Breastropes may be put out to hold her close alongside if there is any wind off the
quay, and to control her on leaving.

LEAVING A WHARF IN A TIDEWAY

A wharf open to a tideway will usually have been built parallel to it.

Single up to one rope upstream, the upstream breastrope and the downstream spring.
When ready to go, slack away or let go the upstream rope and hold on to the downstream spring. The pressure of water between the vessel and the wharf will cause the
upstream end of the ship to move outwards and form a cushion between the wharf
and the stern. Do not let the breastrope go until it is certain that she will not swing off
too quickly. When clear kick engines ahead and let go the downstream spring.

GOING ALONGSIDE ANOTHER VESSEL

If the other vessel is at anchor or on a buoy she is free to swing and will pivot round her
stem. As you close with her the water pressure from your bows will tend to push her

stern away so your approach must not be at too fine an angle or too great a speed. Otherwise in calm weather the method is similar to going alongside a wharf. When alongside good fenders must be used between the vessels.

When letting go it is no good trying to spring the bow or stern out as both ships will swing round the anchored ship's cable. If all lines are let go the two vessels will soon drift apart. If there is any wind let go the forward lines and when both bow have swung apart let go the after lines and go ahead on the engines.

TWIN SCREW VESSELS

Almost all twin screw vessels have out turning propellers, that is a right handed one on the starboard shaft and a left handed one on the port shaft.

If a twin screw vessel is fitted with a single rudder, the streams from the two propellers will pass on each side of the rudder. In this case the rudder has very little power to turn the vessel until she has gathered good headway.

When both propellers turn at the same speed ahead or astern the screw race of one is counter balanced by that of the other. However, if one is going faster than the other or one ahead and the other astern they can be used to great effect in turning the vessel.

Remember that in doing any manoeuvring when vessels are in sight of one another the appropriate signals must be given in accordance with Rule 28 (See Chapter 6).

Any helm orders given must be in a loud clear voice and should be repeated by the man at the wheel.

Chapter Five

British Uniform System of Buoyage and Wreck Marking Systems

The present system of maritime buoyage around the United Kingdom coasts was adopted for use in 1947 by the General Lighthouse Authorities of the United Kingdom. In order to be able to use the system so as to avoid running your ship into danger it is necessary to understand what is meant by the main stream of flood tide.

Figure 5.1 indicates the direction of this main stream of flood and should be carefully studied and memorised. A mariner navigating on our coasts should always be aware of the direction for the area in which he is situated, especially in limited visibility when he may be unsure of his exact position or come up with a buoy unexpectedly.

Starboard Hand—means that side of a channel or route which will be on the RIGHT HAND of the mariner when going with the main stream of flood tide OR when ENTERING a harbour, river or estuary FROM SEAWARD.

Port Hand —means that side which will be on the LEFT HAND of the mariner in identical circumstances.

The main marker buoys used are either conical, can or spherical in shape.

A **CONICAL** buoy shall always be passed on the *starboard hand* when going with the main stream of flood. It should, then, be obvious where the SAFE water is, so it will be understood that to pass through the same water when going against the main stream of flood it will be necessary to leave a conical buoy to port.

A **CAN** buoy shall always be passed on the *port hand* when going with the main stream of flood. To use the same water when bound against the main stream it is left to starboard.

A **SPHERICAL** buoy may be left on either hand when proceeding with the main flood stream or against it, but it is very important to ascertain the topmark carried by this buoy and to know its meaning, which see below under middle ground marks.

Buoys used to mark the sides of channels. See Fig. 5.2

Starboard hand marks will be conical and, black in colour, or for purposes of differentiation, black and white chequers. If they have a topmark it will be a black cone point upwards. For purposes of differentiation it may be a black diamond but this will not be

Fig. 5.1 The Main Stream of Flood Tide

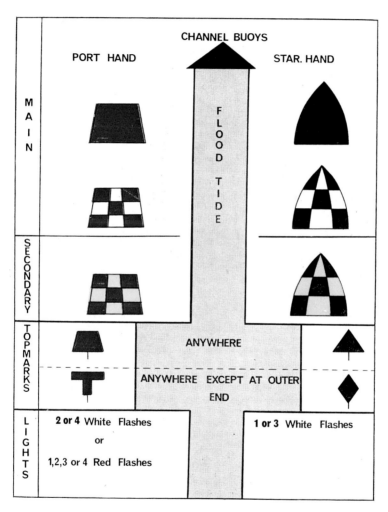

Fig. 5.2 The Uniform System of Buoyage (Lateral)

used on a conical buoy at the entrance to a channel. At night the buoy will show a white light flashing one *or* three.

Port hand marks will be can, and red in colour, or for differentiation, red and white chequers. If they have a topmark it will be a red can. For differentiating it may be a red "T" but will not be used on a can buoy at the entrance to a channel.

At night the buoy will show either a white light flashing two *or* four or a red light showing any number of flashes up to four.

Middle grounds and their marks. See Fig. 5.3

A middle ground is a bank which divides one channel into two channels over the distance between its ends. The two channels may be of equal importance or one may become a secondary channel by reason of its depth and/or breadth.

The ends of a middle ground will be marked by a spherical buoy which it will be remembered may be passed on either hand.

If the *channels* on either side of the middle ground are of *equal importance* the buoy will have red and white horizontal bands. The one at the outer end of the middle ground, that is the end from which the main stream of flood tide is coming, will have a red spherical topmark. The one at the inner end will have a red St. George's Cross as a topmark.

If the *main channel is to the right* the buoy will also have red and white horizontal bands but the topmark will be a red can at the outer end and a red "T" at the inner end. If the *main channel is to the left* when going with the main stream of flood the buoy will have black and white horizontal bands. The topmark on the one at the outer end will be a black cone point upwards and at the inner end a black diamond.

As far as possible the lights on middle ground buoys are distinctive. Neither colour nor rhythm are such as to lead to uncertainty on which side to pass. No colours are used other than white or red.

Various other buoys are in use as illustrated in Figs. 5.3 and 5.4.

Mid channel marks. See Fig. 5.3.

The usual shape is a pillar buoy and if it has a topmark it may be a double cross. They may be passed on either hand but should preferably be left on the port hand.

These marks are to indicate a deep water channel or fairway. Generally speaking they are distinctive and different from the three principal shapes. In colour they are of red and white or black and white vertical stripes. If they carry a topmark it is to be a distinctive shape other than cone, can or sphere. Their lights, if any, are to be different from any neighbouring lights marking the sides of the channel.

Landfall marks. See Fig. 5.4.

These are usually buoys shaped in accordance with the rules for channel marks. They will usually be painted in black and white or red and white vertical stripes. If a light is fitted it is usually of a flashing character. This type of mark is usually placed well to seaward of offshore dangers so that a mariner approaching may fix his position before coming close to those dangers. Marks of this type are usually laid when the dangers are in such a position that the land may not be in sight before reaching them.

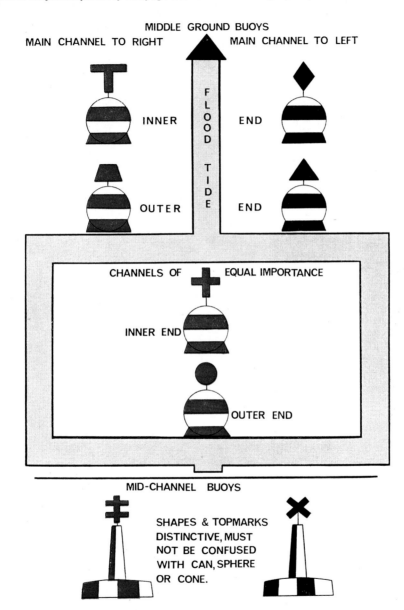

Fig. 5.3 The Uniform System of Buoyage (Lateral)

Isolated danger marks. See Fig. 5.4.

These are buoys spherical in shape painted with deep red and black horizontal bands having a narrow white band in between them. They may carry a spherical topmark painted red, black or half red and half black divided horizontally. They show a white or red flashing light.

Danger zone marks. See Fig. 5.4.

Buoys shaped to indicate the side on which it is safe to pass. Coloured yellow with red St. George's Cross on top giving appearance of red and yellow vertical stripes from all sides. The letters DZ are usually painted on. These buoys are used to mark naval and military practice areas. Outside U.K. waters they may be of another colour.

Quarantine Ground buoys are usually painted yellow and shaped to indicate the side to pass.

Outfall and spoil ground buoys are used to mark the discharging grounds of dredgers. They are yellow and black divided horizontally and shaped to indicate the side to pass. Details of buoys around the U.K. coast are not mentioned in the Admiralty List of Lights although they may be given in the Admiralty Pilot or Sailing Directions. Many buoys are actually listed in Reed's Nautical Almanac. The best reference may be the largest-scale chart of the area concerned but all yachtsmen are advised to consult the NAVEAMS in the Admiralty Notices to Mariners and if they have a radio listen out for SÉCURITÉ messages when at sea.

Light Vessels off the coast of the British Isles are painted red in England and Scotland and black in Ireland and have their name in white on their sides. At night a white light is shown from the forestay and the direction in which the vessel is swinging gives an indication of the tidal flow direction at the time. These vessels must never be approached too closely.

If a Light vessel has moved out of position she will obliterate all her published characteristics and act as follows:

At night she shows an all round red light at each end and also a red and white flare-up light every fifteen minutes. If at anchor she carries her riding light and, if under way she carries her sidelights.

By day she shows a black ball at each end and flies the International Code flags "LO".

In Fog she will sound the normal fog signals for a vessel of her length under way or at anchor as the case may be.

WRECK MARKING SYSTEM

The buoys and vessels used to mark wrecks dangerous to surface navigation are indicated in Fig. 5.4.

All wreck markers are painted green and show green lights. The buoys have a white "W" painted on them and the vessels the word "WRECK" in white on their sides.

Can buoys are to be passed on the port hand when going with the flood stream. Conical buoys are to be passed on the starboard hand when going with the flood stream. Spherical buoys may be passed on either hand.

Wreck marking vessels are not often met with but tragic events in the English Channel near the Varne Bank in 1971 caused an immediate need for them.

The authorities appear to have adapted normal light vessels for this purpose but according to Admiralty Notices to Mariners Nos: 154 and 350 of 1971, which might be obtained and studied, these Wreck Marking Vessels are not showing the marks nor making the fog signals indicated in Figure 5.4.

The Wreck marking vessel to be passed on the port hand does show two green lights vertically at night but her day signal is a green can over a green ball.

The one to be passed on the starboard hand does show three green lights vertically at night but her day signal is a green cone point upwards over two green balls.

Additionally at night a main light on the mast shows green with a character and range which should be seen at some distance.

Similarly the fog signals are diaphones which should give a more definite warning to approaching vessels.

This system of marks and signals may be the one which will be used in future but you should be prepared to meet both until a definite Official Notice is promulgated.

Finally see Fig. 5.5 where a buoyed channel or system of channels is laid out. Start at the bottom left hand corner of the picture and navigate through the buoys to the top centre. Do not try to see the picture as a whole, rather study each mark as you come to it as you would do at sea, act accordingly and then be prepared to sight the next mark.

Always remember that it is possible around the coast of the U.K. to come up with a buoy when you are on a course at right angles, or indeed any angle to the direction of the main stream of flood and you must be prepared to deal with this.

A storm may have put a buoy out of position or destroyed its topmark and birds may have obscured its colour with their droppings.

Chapter Six

The Collision Regulations

INTRODUCTION

The International Regulations for Preventing Collisions at Sea are without doubt the most important item in any book on seamanship and, will most certainly be regarded as such in any examination on this subject.

It is the duty of every Master, Owner and person in charge of a vessel to acquire a thorough knowledge of the International Regulations for Preventing Collisions at Sea and, although there is no statutory requirement to do so, many mariners learn the Rules by heart, as the wording of each is so precise that the slightest deviation from the phraseology could well change the meaning of the rule.

Rules for the purpose of avoiding collision at sea have been in existence for many hundreds of years, but it was not until 1840 that Trinity House drew up a set of Statutory Regulations which were enacted by Parliament in 1846.

The present regulations which came into force on 1st September, 1965, were drawn up by the International Conference on Safety of Life at Sea—at which practically every country in the world is represented.

DUTIES IN CASE OF COLLISION

When a British vessel is involved in a collision, it is essential that a report be made out by the Master and handed to the Customs Officer on arrival at a Port in the United Kingdom. Where there has been loss of life, serious injury or should the vessel have been badly damaged, a signed report should be sent by the Owner or Master to the Department of Trade and Industry Marine Division, as soon as possible after the collision.

The Master of each vessel in a collision is required to render as much assistance as he can to the other vessel and to all persons aboard and to stand by until assistance is no longer necessary. The Masters must each give to the other the name and Port of Registry of their ship and the Ports of departure and arrival and, an entry must be made in the Log Book. It is most essential that the Log Books are properly written-up to include the fullest particulars as they may be required to be used for evidence at a preliminary enquiry or at a formal investigation if it is considered that the collision was due to a wrongful act or negligence by the Master and, also in a Court case where damages may be involved.

MOST IMPORTANT

The following regulations were in force when this book was published in 1971. The next International Conference on Safety of Life at Sea is due to be held in the Autumn of 1972 when new regulations to meet current demands will most probably be submitted. Any new regulations would first have to be agreed by a majority of the Governments concerned and would therefore not come into operation immediately. Readers are, however, advised to keep themselves informed on this matter after October 1972 by contacting: The Information Officer, Inter-governmental Maritime Consultative Organisation, 101 Piccadilly, London, W.1. Tel: 01-499 9040, Extension 61.

INTERNATIONAL REGULATIONS FOR PREVENTING COLLISIONS AT SEA

PART A.—PRELIMINARY AND DEFINITIONS

Rule 1

(*a*) These Rules shall be followed by all vessels and seaplanes upon the high seas and in all waters connected therewith navigable by seagoing vessels, except as provided in Rule 30. Where, as a result of their special construction, it is not possible for seaplanes to comply fully with the provisions of Rules specifying the carrying of lights and shapes, these provisions shall be followed as closely as circumstances permit.

(*b*) **The Rules concerning lights shall be complied with in all weathers from sunset to sunrise, and during such times no other lights shall be exhibited, except such lights as cannot be mistaken for the prescribed lights or impair their visibility or distinctive character, or interfere with the keeping of a proper look-out. The lights prescribed by these Rules may also be exhibited from sunrise to sunset in restricted visibility and in all other circumstances when it is deemed necessary.**

(*c*) In the following Rules, except where the context otherwise requires:—

    (i) the word "vessel" includes every description of water craft, other than a seaplane on the water, used or capable of being used as a means of transportation on water;

    (ii) The word "seaplane" includes a flying boat and any other aircraft designed to manoeuvre on the water;

    (iii) The term "power-driven vessel" means any vessel propelled by machinery;

    (iv) every power-driven vessel which is under sail and not under power is to be considered a sailing vessel, and every vessel under power, whether under sail or not, is to be considered a power-driven vessel;

    (v) a vessel or seaplane on the water is **"under way"** when she is not at anchor, or made fast to the shore, or aground;

    (vi) the term "height above the hull" means height above the uppermost continuous deck;

    (vii) the length and breadth of a vessel shall be her length overall and largest breadth;

    (viii) the length and span of a seaplane shall be its maximum length and span as shown in its certificate of airworthiness, or as determined by measurement in the absence of such certificate;

    (ix) vessels shall be deemed to be in sight of one another only when one can be observed visually from the other;

(x) the word **"visible"**, when applied to lights, means visible on a dark night with a clear atmosphere;

(xi) **the term "short blast" means a blast of about one second's duration;**

(xii) **the term "prolonged blast" means a blast of from four to six seconds duration;**

(xiii) the word "whistle" means any appliance capable of producing the prescribed short and prolonged blasts;

(xiv) the term "engaged in fishing" means fishing with nets, lines or trawls but does not include fishing with trolling lines.

PART B.—LIGHTS AND SHAPES

Rule 2

Lights for Power Vessels or Seaplanes

(*a*) **A power-driven vessel when under way** shall carry:—

(i) On or in front of the foremast, or if a vessel without a foremast then in the forepart of the vessel, a **white light** so constructed as to show an unbroken light over an arc of the horizon of 225° (20 points of the compass), so fixed as to show the light 112½° (10 points) on each side of the vessel, that is, from right ahead to 22½° (two points) abaft the beam on either side, and of such a character as to be visible at a distance of at least five miles.

(ii) Either forward or abaft the white light mentioned in sub-section (i) a **second white light** similar in construction and character to that light. Vessels of less than 150 feet in length, shall not be required to carry this second white light but may do so.

(iii) These two white lights shall be so placed in a line with and over the keel that one shall be at least 15 feet higher than the other and in such a position that the forward **light shall always be shown lower than the after one.** The horizontal distance between the two white lights shall be at least three times the vertical distance. The lower of these two white lights or, if only one is carried, then that light shall be placed at a height above the hull of not less than 20 feet, and, if the breadth of the vessel exceeds 20 feet, then at a height above the hull not less than such breadth, so however that the light need not be placed at a greater height above the hull than 40 feet. In all circumstances the light or lights, as the case may be, shall be so placed as to be clear of and above all other lights and obstructing superstructures.

(iv) On the **starboard side a green light** so constructed as to show an unbroken light over an arc of the horizon of 112½° (10 points of the compass), so fixed as to show the light from right ahead to 22½° (two points) abaft the beam on the starboard side, and of such a character as to be visible at a distance of at least two miles.

(v) On the **port side a red light** so constructed as to show an unbroken light over an arc of the horizon of 112½° (10 points of the compass), so fixed as to show the light from right ahead to 22½° (two points) abaft the beam on the port side, and of such a character as to be visible at a distance of a least two miles.

(vi) The said green and red sidelights shall be fitted with inboard screens projecting at least three feet forward from the light, so as to prevent these lights from being seen across the bows.

(*b*) A **seaplane under way on the water** shall carry:—

   (i) In the forepart amidships where it can best be seen a **white light,** so constructed as to show an unbroken light over an arc of the horizon of 220° of the compass, so fixed as to show the light 110° on each side of the seaplane, namely, from right ahead to 20° abaft the beam on either side, and of such a character as to be visible at a distance of at least three miles.

   (ii) On the right or **starboard wing tip a green light,** so constructed as to show an unbroken light over an arc of the horizon of 110° of the compass, so fixed as to show the light from right ahead to 20° abaft the beam on the starboard side and of such a character as to be visible at a distance of at least two miles.

   (iii) On the left or **port wing tip a red light,** so constructed as to show an unbroken light over an arc of the horizon of 110° of the compass, so fixed as to show the light from right ahead to 20° abaft the beam on the port side, and of such a character as to be visible at a distance of at least two miles.

Rule 3

Lights for Power Vessels or Seaplanes, Towing or Pushing

(*a*) A power-driven vessel when towing or pushing another vessel or seaplane shall, in addition to her sidelights, carry two white lights in a vertical line one over the other, not less than six feet apart, and when **towing** and **the length of the tow,** measuring from the stern of the towing vessel to the stern of the last vessel towed, **exceeds 600 feet,** shall carry **three white lights** in a vertical line one over the other, so that the upper and lower lights shall be the same distance from, and not less than six feet above or below the middle light. Each of these lights shall be of the same construction and character and one of them shall be carried in the same position as the white light prescribed in Rule 2 (*a*) (i). None of these lights shall be carried at a height of less than 14 feet above the hull. In a vessel with a single mast, such lights may be carried on the mast.

(*b*) The towing vessel shall also show either the stern light specified in Rule 10 or in lieu of that light a small white light abaft the funnel or aftermast for the tow to steer by, but such light shall not be visible forward of the beam.

(*c*) **Between sunrise and sunset a power-driven vessel engaged in towing, if the length of tow exceeds 600 feet, shall carry, where it can best be seen, a black diamond shape at least two feet in diameter.**

(*d*) A seaplane on the water, when towing one or more seaplanes or vessels, shall carry the lights prescribed in Rule 2 (*b*) (i), (ii) and (iii); and, in addition, she shall carry a second white light of the same construction and character as the white light mentioned in Rule 2 (*b*) (i), and in a vertical line at least six feet above or below such light.

Rule 4

Vessels not under Command

(*a*) A vessel which is not under command shall carry, **where they can best be seen,** and, if a power-driven vessel, in lieu of the lights required by Rule 2 (*a*) (i) and (ii),

two red lights in a vertical line one over the other not less than six feet apart, and of such a character as to be visible all round the horizon at a distance of at least two miles. By day, she shall carry in a vertical line one over the other not less than six feet apart, **where they can best be seen, two black balls or shapes** each not less than two feet in diameter.

(*b*) A seaplane on the water which is not under command may carry, where they can best be seen, and in lieu of the light prescribed in Rule 2 (*b*) (i) two red lights in a vertical line, one over the other, not less than three feet apart, and of such a character as to be visible all round the horizon at a distance of at least two miles, and may by day carry in a vertical line one over the other not less than three feet apart, where they can best be seen, two black balls or shapes, each not less than two feet in diameter.

(*c*) **A vessel engaged in laying or in picking up a submarine cable** or **navigation mark,** or a vessel engaged in surveying or underwater operations, or a vessel engaged in replenishment at sea, or in the launching or recovery of aircraft when from the nature of her work she is unable to get out of the way of approaching vessels, shall carry, in lieu of the lights specified in Rule 2 (*a*) (i) and (ii), or Rule 7 (*a*) (i), **three lights in a vertical line** one over the other so that the upper and lower lights shall be the same distance from, and not less than six feet above or below, the middle light. The highest and lowest of these lights shall be red, and the middle light shall be white, and they shall be of such a character as to be visible all round the horizon at a distance of at least two miles. By day, she shall carry in a vertical line one over the other not less than six feet apart, where they can best be seen, **three shapes** each not less than two feet in diameter, of which the highest and lowest shall be globular in shape and red in colour, and the middle one diamond in shape and white.

(*d*) (i) A vessel engaged in **minesweeping operations** shall carry at the fore truck a **green** light, and at the end or ends of the fore yard on the side or sides on which danger exists, another such light or lights. These lights shall be carried in addition to the light prescribed in Rule 2 (*a*) (i) or Rule 7 (*a*) (i), as appropriate, and shall be of such a character as to be visible all round the horizon at a distance of at least two miles. By day she shall carry **black balls,** not less than two feet in diameter, in the same position as the green lights.

(ii) The showing of these lights or balls indicates that it is **dangerous for other vessels to approach** closer than 3,000 feet astern of the minesweeper or 1,500 feet on the side or sides on which danger exists.

(*e*) The vessels and seaplanes referred to in this Rule, when not making way through the water, shall show neither the coloured sidelights not the stern light **but when making way they shall carry them.**

(*f*) The lights and shapes prescribed in this Rule are to be taken by other vessels and seaplanes as signals that the vessel or seaplane showing them is not under command **and cannot therefore get out of the way.**

(*g*) These signals are **not** signals of vessels in distress and requiring assistance. Such signals are contained in Rule 31.

Rule 5

Lights for Sailing Vessels and Vessels Towed

(*a*) A **sailing vessel** under way and **any vessel or seaplane being towed** shall carry the same lights as are prescribed in Rule 2 for a power-driven vessel or a seaplane under way, respectively, with the exception of the white lights specified therein, which they shall never carry. They shall also carry stern lights as specified in Rule 10, provided that vessels towed, except the last vessel of a tow, may carry, in lieu of such stern light, a small white light as specified in Rule 3 (*b*).

(*b*) **In addition to the lights prescribed in section (*a*), a sailing vessel may carry on the top of the foremast two lights in a vertical line one over the other, sufficiently separated so as to be clearly distinguished. The upper light shall be red** and the **lower light shall be green.** Both lights shall be constructed and fixed as prescribed in Rule 2 (*a*) (i) and shall be visible at a distance of at least two miles.

(*c*) A **vessel being pushed** ahead shall carry, at the forward end, on the starboard side a green light and on the port side a red light, which shall have the same characteristics as the lights described in Rule 2 (*a*) (iv) and (v) and shall be screened as provided in Rule 2 (*a*) (vi), provided that any number of vessels pushed ahead in a group shall be lighted as one vessel.

(*d*) Between sunrise and sunset a **vessel being towed,** if the length of the tow exceeds 600 feet, **shall carry** where it can best be seen a **black diamond** shape at least two feet in diameter.

Rule 6

Lights for Small Vessels

(*a*) When it is not possible on account of bad weather or other sufficient cause to fix the green and red sidelights, these lights shall be kept at hand lighted and ready for immediate use, and shall, on the approach of or to other vessels, be exhibited on their respective sides in sufficient time to prevent collision, in such manner as to make them most visible, and so that the green light shall not be seen on the port side nor the red light on the starboard side, nor, if practicable, more than $22\frac{1}{2}°$ (two points) abaft the beam on their respective sides.

(*b*) To make the use of these portable lights more certain and easy, the lanterns containing them shall each be painted outside with the colour of the lights they respectively contain, and shall be provided with proper screens.

Rule 7

Lights for Small Vessels

Power-driven vessels of less than 65 feet in length, vessels under oars or sails of less than 40 feet in length, and rowing boats, when under way shall not be required to carry the lights mentioned in Rules 2, 3 and 5, but if they do not carry them they shall be provided with the following lights:—

(*a*) **Power-driven vessels of less than 65 feet in length,** except as provided in sections (*b*) and (*c*), shall carry:—

    (i) In the forepart of the vessel, where it can best be seen, and at a height above the gunwale of not less than nine feet, a white light constructed and fixed as prescribed in Rule 2 (*a*) (i) and of such a character as to be visible at a distance of at least three miles.

(ii) Green and red sidelights constructed and fixed as prescribed in Rule 2 (*a*) (iv) and (v), and of such a character as to be visible at a distance of at least one mile, or a combined lantern showing a green light and a red light from right ahead to $22\frac{1}{2}°$ (two points) abaft the beam on their respective sides. Such lantern shall be carried not less than three feet below the white light.

(*b*) [**Power-driven vessels of less than 65 feet in length when towing or pushing another vessel** shall carry:—

    (i) In addition to the sidelights or the combined lantern prescribed in section (*a*) (ii) two white lights in a vertical line, one over the other not less than four feet apart. Each of these lights shall be of the same construction and character as the white light prescribed in section (*a*) (i) and one of them shall be carried in the same position. In a vessel with a single mast such lights may be carried on the mast.

    (ii) Either a stern light as prescribed in Rule 10 or in lieu of that light a small white light abaft the funnel or aftermast for the tow to steer by, but such light shall not be visible forward of the beam.

(*c*) **Power-driven vessels of less than 40 feet in length** may carry the white light at a less height than nine feet above the gunwale but it shall be carried not less than three feet above the sidelights or the combined lantern prescribed in section (*a*) (ii).

(*d*) **Vessels of less than 40 feet in length, under oars or sails,** except as provided in section (*f*), shall, if they do not carry the sidelights, carry, where it can best be seen a lantern showing a green light on one side and a red light on the other, of such a character as to be visible at a distance of at least one mile, and so fixed that the green light shall not be seen on the port side, nor the red light on the starboard side. Where it is not possible to fix this light, it shall be kept ready for immediate use and shall be exhibited in sufficient time to prevent collision and so that the green light shall not be seen on the port side nor the red light on the starboard.

(*e*)] The vessels referred to in this Rule **when being towed** shall carry the sidelights or the combined lantern prescribed in sections (*a*) or (*d*) of this Rule, as appropriate, and a stern light as prescribed in Rule 10, or, except the last vessel of the tow, a small white light as prescribed in section (*b*) (ii). **When being pushed ahead** they shall carry at the forward end the sidelights or combined lantern prescribed in sections (*a*) or (*d*) of this Rule, as appropriate, provided that any number of vessels referred to in this Rule when pushed ahead in a group shall be lighted as one vessel under this Rule unless the overall length of the group exceeds 65 feet when the provisions of Rule 5 (*c*) shall apply.

(*f*) **Small rowing boats,** whether under oars or sail, shall only be required to have ready at hand an electric torch or a lighted lantern showing a **white** light, which shall be exhibited in sufficient time to prevent collision.

(*g*) **The vessels and boats referred to in this Rule shall not be required to carry the lights or shapes prescribed in Rules 4 (*a*) and 11 (*e*), and the size of their day signals may be less than is prescribed in Rules 4 (*c*) and 11 (*c*).**

Rule 8

Lights for Pilot Vessels

(*a*) **A power-driven pilot-vessel when engaged on pilotage duty and under way:—**

   (i) Shall carry a **white light at the masthead** at a height of not less than 20 feet above the hull, visible all round the horizon at a distance of at least three miles and at a distance of **eight feet below it a red light** similar in construction and character. If such a vessel is of less than 65 feet in length she may carry the white light at a height of not less than nine feet above the gunwale and the red light at a distance of four feet below the white light.

   (ii) Shall carry the sidelights or lanterns prescribed in Rule 2 (*a*) (iv) and (v) or Rule 7 (*a*) (ii) or (*d*), as appropriate, and the stern light prescribed in Rule 10.

   (iii) Shall show one or more **flare-up lights** at intervals not exceeding 10 minutes. An intermittent white light visible all round the horizon may be used in lieu of flare-up lights.

(*b*) **A sailing pilot-vessel when engaged on pilotage duty and under way:—**

   (i) Shall carry a **white light at the masthead** visible all round the horizon at a distance of at least three miles.

   (ii) Shall be provided with the sidelights or lantern prescribed in Rules 5 (*a*) or 7 (*d*), as appropriate, and shall, on the near approach of or to other vessels, have such lights ready for use, and shall show them at short intervals to indicate the direction in which she is heading, but the green light shall not be shown on the port side nor the red light on the starboard side. She shall also carry the stern light prescribed in Rule 10.

   (iii) Shall show one or more **flare-up lights** at intervals not exceeding 10 minutes.

(*c*) A pilot-vessel when engaged on pilotage duty and **not under way** shall carry the lights and show the flares prescribed in sections (*a*) (i) and (iii) or (*b*) (i) and (iii), as appropriate, and if at anchor shall also carry the anchor lights prescribed in Rule 11.

(*d*) A pilot-vessel when not engaged on pilotage duty shall show the lights or shapes for a similar vessel of her length.

Rule 9

Lights for Fishing Vessels

(*a*) **Fishing vessels when not engaged in fishing shall show the lights or shapes prescribed for similar vessels of their length.**

(*b*) **Vessels engaged in fishing, when under way or at anchor, shall show only the lights and shapes prescribed in this Rule, which lights and shapes shall be visible at a distance of at least two miles.**

(*c*)   (i) Vessels when engaged in **trawling,** by which is meant the dragging of a dredge net or other apparatus through the water, **shall carry two lights in a vertical line, one over the other,** not less than four feet nor more than 12 feet apart. **The upper of these lights shall be green and the lower light white** and each shall be visible all round the horizon. The lower of these two lights shall be carried at a height above the sidelights not less than twice the distance between the two vertical lights.

(ii) Such vessels may in addition carry a white light similar in construction to the white light prescribed in Rule 2 (*a*) (i) but such light shall be carried lower than and abaft the all-round green and white lights.

(*d*) Vessels when engaged in **fishing**, except vessels engaged in trawling, shall carry the lights prescribed in section (*c*) (i) except that **the upper of the two vertical lights shall be red.** Such vessels if of less than 40 feet in length may carry the red light at a height of not less than nine feet above the gunwale and the white light not less than three feet below the red light.

(*e*) Vessels referred to in sections (*c*) and (*d*), **when making way through the water, shall carry the sidelights or lanterns** prescribed in Rule 2 (*a*) (iv) and (v) or Rule 7 (*a*) (ii) or (*d*), as appropriate, and the stern light prescribed in Rule 10. **When not making way through the water they shall show neither the sidelights nor the stern light.**

(*f*) Vessels referred to in section (*d*) with outlying gear extending more than 500 feet horizontally into the seaway shall carry an additional all-round white light at a horizontal distance of not less than six feet nor more than 20 feet away from the vertical lights in the direction of the outlying gear. This additional white light shall be placed at a height not exceeding that of the white light prescribed in section (*c*) (i) and not lower than the sidelights.

(*g*) In addition to the lights which they are required by this Rule to carry, **vessels engaged in fishing** may, if necessary in order to attract the attention of an approaching vessel, **use a flare-up light,** or may direct the beam of their searchlight in the direction of a danger threatening the approaching vessel, in such a way as not to embarrass other vessels. They may also use **working lights** but fishermen shall take into account that specially bright or insufficiently screened working lights may impair the visibility and distinctive character of the lights prescribed in this Rule.

(*h*) **By day vessels when engaged in fishing** shall indicate their occupation by displaying where it can best be seen a black shape consisting of **two cones** each not less than two feet in diameter with their **points together one above the other. Such vessels if of less than 65 feet in length may substitute a basket for such black shape.** If their outlying gear extends more than 500 feet horizontally into the seaway vessels engaged in fishing shall display in addition **one black conical shape, point upwards,** in the direction of the outlying gear.

Note:—Vessels fishing with trolling lines are not "engaged" in fishing as defined in Rule 1 (c) xiv

Rule 10

Stern Light

(*a*) Except where otherwise provided in these Rules a **vessel when under way shall carry at her stern a white light,** so constructed that it shall show an unbroken light over an arc of the horizon of 135° (12 points of the compass), so fixed as to show the light 67½° (six points) from right aft on each side of the vessel, and of such a character as to be visible at a distance of at least two miles.

(*b*) In a small vessel, if it is not possible on account of bad weather or other sufficient cause for this light to be fixed, an electric torch or a lighted lantern showing a white light shall be kept at hand ready for use and shall, on the approach of an overtaking vessel, be shown in sufficient time to prevent collision.

(*c*) A seaplane on the water when under way shall carry on her tail a white light, so constructed as to show an unbroken light over an arc of the horizon of 140° of the compass, so fixed as to show the light 70° from right aft on each side of the seaplane, and of such a character as to be visible at a distance of at least two miles.

Rule 11

Lights for Vessels at Anchor

(a) **A vessel of less than 150 feet in length, when at anchor,** shall carry in the forepart of the vessel, where it can best be seen, a **white** light visible all round the horizon at a distance of at least two miles. Such a vessel **may also carry a second white light** in the position prescribed in section (b) of this Rule but shall not be required to do so. The second white light, if carried, shall be visible at a distance of at least two miles and so placed as to be as far as possible visible all round the horizon.

(b) **A vessel of 150 feet or more in length,** when at anchor, shall carry near the stem of the vessel, at a height of not less than 20 feet above the hull, **one** such light, and at or near the stern of the vessel and at such a height that it shall be not less than 15 feet lower than the forward light, **another** such light. Both these lights shall be visible at a distance of at least three miles and so placed as to be as far as possible visible all round the horizon.

(c) **Between sunrise and sunset every vessel when at anchor shall carry in the forepart of the vessel, where it can best be seen, one black ball not less than two feet in diameter.**

(d) A vessel engaged in laying or in picking up a submarine cable or navigation mark, or a vessel engaged in surveying or underwater operations, when at anchor, shall carry the lights or shapes prescribed in Rule 4 (c) in addition to those prescribed in the appropriate preceding sections of this Rule.

(e) **A vessel aground** shall carry the light or lights prescribed in sections (a) or (b) and the two red lights prescribed in Rule 4 (a). By day she shall carry, where they can best be seen, **three black balls,** each not less than two feet in diameter, placed in a vertical line one over the other, not less than six feet apart.

(f) A seaplane on the water under 150 feet in length, when at anchor, shall carry, where it can best be seen, a white light, visible all round the horizon at a distance of at least two miles.

(g) A seaplane on the water 150 feet or upwards in length, when at anchor, shall carry, where they can best be seen, a white light forward and a white light aft, both lights visible all round the horizon at a distance of at least three miles; and, in addition, if the seaplane is more than 150 feet in span, a white light on each side to indicate the maximum span, and visible, so far as practicable, all round the horizon at a distance of one mile.

(h) A seaplane aground shall carry an anchor light or lights as prescribed in sections (f) and (g), and in addition may carry two red lights in a vertical line, at least three feet apart, so placed as to be visible all round the horizon.

Rule 12

Signal to Attract Attention

Every vessel or seaplane on the water may, if necessary **in order to attract attention,** in addition to the lights which she is by these Rules required to carry, show a flare-up light or use a detonating or other efficient sound signal that cannot be mistaken for any signal authorised elsewhere under these Rules.

Rule 13

Special Rules

(*a*) Nothing in these Rules shall interfere with the operation of any special rules made by the Government of any nation with respect to additional station and signal lights for ships of war, for vessels sailing under convoy, for fishing vessels engaged in fishing as a fleet, or for seaplanes on the water.

(*b*) Whenever the Government concerned shall have determined that a naval or other military vessel or waterborne seaplane of special construction or purpose cannot comply fully with the provisions of any of these Rules with respect to the number, position, range of arc of visibility of lights or shapes, without interfering with the military function of the vessel or seaplane, such vessel or seaplane shall comply with such other provisions in regard to the number, position, range or arc of visibility of lights or shapes as her Government shall have determined to be the closest possible compliance with these Rules in respect of that vessel or seaplane.

Rule 14

Vessel under Sail—Using Power also
A vessel proceeding under sail, when also being propelled by machinery, shall carry in the daytime forward, where it can best be seen, one black conical shape, point downwards, not less than two feet in diameter at its base.

PART C.—
SOUND SIGNALS AND CONDUCT IN RESTRICTED VISIBILITY
Preliminary

(1) **The possession of information obtained from radar does not relieve any vessel of the obligation of conforming strictly with the Rules and, in particular, the obligations contained in Rules 15 and 16.**

(2) The Annex to the Rules contains recommendations intended to assist in the use of radar as an aid to avoiding collision in restricted visibility.

Rule 15

Sound Signals for Fog

(*a*) **A power-driven vessel of 40 feet or more in length** shall be provided with an efficient whistle, sounded by steam or by some substitute for steam, so placed that the sound, may not be intercepted by any obstruction, and with an efficient fog-horn, to be sounded by mechanical means, and also with an efficient bell. A sailing vessel of 40 feet or more in length shall be provided with a similar fog-horn and bell.

(*b*) All signals prescribed in this Rule for vessels under way shall be given:—
　　(i) by power-driven vessels on the whistle;
　　(ii) by sailing vessels on the fog-horn;
　　(iii) by vessels towed on the whistle or fog-horn.

(*c*) In **fog, mist, falling snow, heavy rainstorms, or any other condition similarly restricting visibility, whether by day or night,** the signals prescribed in this Rule shall be used as follows:—

(i) **A power-driven vessel making way through the water,** shall sound at intervals of not more than two minutes a **prolonged blast.**

(ii) **A power-driven vessel under way, but stopped** and making no way through the water, shall sound at intervals of not more than two minutes **two prolonged blasts,** with an interval of about one second between them.

(iii) **A sailing vessel under way** shall sound, at intervals of not more than one minute, when on the starboard tack **one blast,** when on the port tack **two blasts in succession,** and when with the wind abaft the beam **three blasts in succession.**

(iv) **A vessel when at anchor** shall at intervals of not more than one minute **ring the bell rapidly for about five seconds.** In vessels of more than 350 feet in length the **bell** shall be sounded in the **forepart** of the vessel, and in addition there shall be sounded in the **after** part of the vessel, at intervals of not more than one minute for about five seconds, **a gong or other instrument,** the tone and sounding of which cannot be confused with that of the bell. **Every vessel at anchor may in addition, in accordance with Rule 12, sound three blasts in succession, namely, one short, one prolonged, and one short blast, to give warning of her position and of the possibility of collision to an approaching vessel.**

(v) **A vessel when towing, a vessel engaged in laying or in picking up a submarine cable or navigation mark, and a vessel under way which is unable to get out of the way of an approaching vessel** through being not under command or unable to manoeuvre as required by these Rules shall, instead of the signals prescribed in subsections (i), (ii) and (iii) sound, at intervals, of not more than one minute, three blasts in succession, namely **one prolonged blast followed by two short blasts.**

(vi) **A vessel towed,** or, if more than one vessel is towed, only the last vessel of the tow, if manned, shall, at intervals of not more than one minute, sound four blasts in succession, namely, **one prolonged blast followed by three short blasts.** When practicable, this signal shall be made immediately after the signal made by the towing vessel.

(vii) **A vessel aground shall give the bell signal and if required, the gong signal, prescribed in sub-section (iv) and shall, in addition, give three separate and distinct strokes on the bell immediately before and after such rapid ringing of the bell.**

(viii) **A vessel engaged in fishing when under way or at anchor** shall at intervals of not more than one minute sound the signal prescribed in sub-section (v). A vessel when fishing with trolling lines and under way shall sound the signals prescribed in sub-sections (i), (ii) or (iii) as may be appropriate.

(ix) **A vessel of less than 40 feet in length, a rowing boat, or a seaplane on the water,** shall not be obliged to give the above-mentioned signals, but if she does not, she shall **make some other efficient sound signal** at intervals of not more than one minute.

(x) **A power-driven pilot-vessel when engaged on pilotage duty may, in addition to** the signals prescribed in sub-sections (i), (ii) and (iv) **sound an identity signal consisting of four short blasts.**

Rule 16

Speed to be moderate in fog

(*a*) **Every vessel,** or seaplane when taxi-ing on the water, shall in fog, mist, falling snow, heavy rainstorms or any other condition similarly restricting visibility, **go at a moderate speed,** having careful regard to the existing circumstances and conditions.

(*b*) A **power-driven vessel** hearing, apparently forward of her beam, the fog-signal of a vessel **the position of which is not ascertained,** shall, so far as the circumstances of the case admit, **stop her engines,** and then navigate with caution until danger of collision is over.

(*c*) **A power-driven vessel which detects the presence of another vessel forward of her beam before hearing her fog-signal or sighting her visually may take early and substantial action to avoid a close quarters situation but, if this cannot be avoided, she shall, so far as the circumstances of the case admit, stop her engines in proper time to avoid collision and then navigate with caution until danger of collision is over.**

PART D.—STEERING AND SAILING RULES

Preliminary,—Risk of Collision

(1) **In obeying and construing these Rules, any action taken should be positive, in ample time, and with due regard to the observance of good seamanship.**

(2) **Risk of collision can, when circumstances permit, be ascertained by carefully watching the compass bearing of an approaching vessel. If the bearing does not appreciably change, such risk should be deemed to exist.**

(3) *Mariners should bear in mind that seaplanes in the act of landing or taking off, or operating under adverse weather conditions, may be unable to change their intended action at the last moment.*

(4) **Rules 17 to 24 apply only to vessels in sight of one another.**

Rule 17

Two Sailing Vessels meeting

(*a*) **When two sailing vessels are approaching one another,** so as to involve risk of collision, one of them shall keep out of the way of the other, as follows:—

    (i) **When each has the wind on a different side, the vessel which has the wind on the port side shall keep out of the way of the other.**

    (ii) **When both have the wind on the same side, the vessel which is to windward shall keep out of the way of the vessel which is to leeward.**

(*b*) For the purposes of this Rule **the windward side shall be deemed to be the side opposite to that on which the mainsail is carried** or, in the case of a square-rigged vessel, the side opposite to that on which the largest fore-and-aft sail is carried.

Rule 18

Two Power Vessels meeting

(*a*) **When two power-driven vessels are meeting end on, or nearly end on, so as to involve risk of collision, each shall alter her course to starboard, so that each may pass on the**

port side of the other. This Rule only applies to cases where vessels are meeting end on, or nearly end on, in such a manner as to involve risk of collision, and does not apply to two vessels which must, if both keep on their respective courses, pass clear of each other. **The only cases to which it does apply** are when each of two vessels is end on, or nearly end on, to the other; in other words, to cases in which, by day, each vessel sees the masts of the other in a line, or nearly in a line, with her own; and by night, to cases in which each vessel is in such a position as to see both the sidelights of the other.

It does not apply, by day, to cases in which a vessel sees another ahead crossing her own course; or by night, to cases where the red light of one vessel is opposed to the red light of the other or where the green light of one vessel is opposed to the green light of the other or where a red light without a green light or a green light without a red light is seen ahead, or where both green and red lights are seen anywhere but ahead.

(*b*) For the purposes of this Rule and Rules 19 to 29 inclusive, except Rule 20 (*b*) and Rule 28, a seaplane on the water shall be deemed to be a vessel, and the expression "power-driven vessel" shall be construed accordingly.

Rule 19

Two Power Vessels Crossing

When two power-driven vessels are **crossing,** so as to involve risk collision, the vessel which has the other **on her starboard side** shall keep out of the way of the other.

Rule 20

Power and Sailing Vessels meeting

(*a*) When a power-driven vessel and a sailing vessel are proceeding in such directions as to involve risk of collision, except as provided for in Rules 24 and 26, the **power-driven vessel shall keep out of the way of the sailing vessel.**

(*b*) **This Rule shall not give to a sailing vessel the right to hamper, in a narrow channel, the safe passage of a power-driven vessel which can navigate only inside such channel.**

(*c*) A seaplane on the water shall, in general, keep well clear of all vessels and avoid impeding their navigation. In circumstances, however, where risk of collision exists, she shall comply with these Rules.

Rule 21

Vessel to keep course and speed

Where by any of these Rules one of two vessels is to keep out of the way, the other shall keep her course and speed. **When, from any cause, the latter vessel finds herself so close that collision cannot be avoided by the action of the giving-away vessel alone, she also shall take such action as will best aid to avert collision (see Rules 27 and 29)**

Rule 22

Vessels to avoid crossing ahead

Every vessel which is directed by these Rules to keep out of the way of another vessel shall, so far as possible, take positive early action to comply with this obligation and shall, if the circumstances of the case admit, **avoid crossing ahead of the other.**

Rule 23

Vessels to alter speed

Every power-driven vessel which is directed by these Rules to keep out of the way of another vessel shall, on approaching her, if necessary, **slacken her speed or stop or reverse.**

Rule 24

Vessel overtaking another

(*a*) **Notwithstanding anything contained in these Rules, every vessel overtaking any other shall keep out of the way of the overtaken vessel.**

(*b*) Every vessel coming up with another vessel from any direction more than $22\frac{1}{2}°$ (two points) abaft her beam, i.e., in such a position, with reference to the vessel which she is overtaking, that at night she would be unable to see either of that vessel's sidelights, shall be deemed to be an overtaking vessel; and no subsequent alteration of the bearing between the two vessels shall make the overtaking vessel a crossing vessel within the meaning of these Rules, or relieve her of the duty of keeping clear of the overtaken vessel until she is finally past and clear.

(*c*) If the overtaking vessel cannot determine with certainty whether she is forward of or abaft this direction from the other vessel, she shall **assume that she is an overtaking vessel and keep out of the way.**

Rule 25

Power Vessels in narrow channels

(*a*) **In a narrow channel every power-driven vessel when proceeding along the course of the channel shall, when it is safe and practicable, keep to that side of the fairway or mid-channel which lies on the starboard side of such vessel.**

(*b*) **Whenever a power-driven vessel is nearing a bend in a channel** where a vessel approaching from the other direction cannot be seen, such power-driven vessel, when she shall have arrived within one-half ($\frac{1}{2}$) mile of the bend, shall give a signal by one **prolonged blast of her whistle,** which signal shall be answered by a similar blast given by any approaching power-driven vessel that may be within hearing around the bend. Regardless of whether an approaching vessel on the farther side of the bend is heard, such bend shall be rounded with alertness and caution.

(*c*) **In a narrow channel a power-driven vessel of less than 65 feet in length shall not hamper the safe passage of a vessel which can navigate only inside such channel.**

Rule 26

Vessels to avoid Fishing Vessels

All vessels not engaged in fishing, except vessels to which the provisions of Rule 4 apply, shall, when under way, keep out of the way of vessels engaged in fishing. This Rule shall not give to any vessel engaged in fishing the right of obstructing a fairway used by vessels other than fishing vessels.

Rule 27

Special Circumstances

In obeying and construing these Rules due regard shall be had to all dangers of navigation and collision, and to any special circumstances, including the limitations of the craft involved, which may render a departure from the above Rules necessary in order to avoid immediate danger.

PART E.—
SOUND SIGNALS FOR VESSELS IN SIGHT OF ONE ANOTHER

Rule 28

Sound Signals for Power Vessels

(*a*) **When vessels are in sight of one another, a power-driven vessel under way,** in taking any course authorised or required by these Rules, shall indicate that course by the following signals on her whistle namely:—
      One short blast to mean "I am altering my course to starboard".
      Two short blasts to mean "I am altering my course to port".
      Three short blasts to mean "My engines are going astern".

(*b*) Whenever a **power-driven vessel** which, under these Rules, is to keep her course and speed, is in sight of another vessel **and is in doubt whether sufficient action is being taken by the other vessel to avert collision, she may indicate such doubt by giving at least five short and rapid blasts on the whistle.** The giving of such a signal shall not relieve a vessel of her obligations under Rules 27 and 29 or any other Rule, or of her duty to indicate any action taken under these Rules by giving the appropriate sound signals laid down in this Rule.

(*c*) **Any whistle signal mentioned in this Rule may be further indicated by a visual signal consisting of a white light** visible all round the horizon at a distance of at least five miles, and so devised that it will operate simultaneously and in conjunction with the whistle-sounding mechanism and remain lighted and visible during the same period as the sound signal.

(*d*) Nothing in these Rules shall interfere with the operation of any special rules made by the Government of any nation with respect to the use of additional whistle signals between ships of war or vessels sailing under convoy.

PART F.—**MISCELLANEOUS**

Rule 29

The Ordinary Practice of Seamen

Nothing in these Rules shall exonerate any vessel, or the owner, master or crew thereof, from the consequences of any neglect to carry lights or signals, or of any neglect to keep a proper look-out, or of the neglect of any precaution which may be required by the ordinary practice of seamen or by the special circumstances of the case.

Rule 30

Reservations of Rules for Harbours and Inland Navigation

Nothing in these Rules shall interfere with the operation of a special rule duly made by local authority relative to the navigation of any harbour, river, lake, or inland water, including a reserved seaplane area.

Rule 31

Distress Signals

When a vessel or seaplane on the water is in distress and requires assistance from other vessels or from the shore, the following shall be the signals to be used or displayed by her, either together or separately, namely:—

    (i) A **gun** or other explosive signal fired at intervals of about a minute.

   (ii) A **continuous sounding** with any fog-signal apparatus.

  (iii) Rockets or shells, throwing **red** stars fired one at a time at short intervals.

  (iv) A signal made by radiotelegraphy or by any other signalling method consisting of the group . . . — — — . . . (SOS) in the Morse Code.

   (v) A signal sent by radiotelephony consisting of the spoken word **"Mayday"**.

  (vi) The International Code Signal of distress indicated by **N.C.**

 (vii) A signal consisting of a **square flag having above or below it a ball** or anything resembling a ball.

(viii) **Flames** on the vessel (as from a burning tar barrel, oil barrel, etc.).

  (ix) A rocket parachute flare showing a **red** light.

   (x) A smoke signal giving off a volume of orange-coloured smoke.

  (xi) Slowly and repeatedly raising and lowering arms outstretched to each side.

Note.—**Vessels in distress may use the radiotelegraph alarm signal or the radiotelephone alarm signal to secure attention to distress calls and messages.** *The radiotelegraph alarm signal, which is designed to actuate the radiotelegraph auto alarms of vessels so fitted, consists of a series of twelve dashes, sent in one minute, the duration of each dash being four seconds, and the duration of the interval between two consecutive dashes being one second. The radiotelephone alarm signal consists of two tones transmitted alternately over periods of from* 30 *seconds to one minute.* **The use of any of the foregoing signals, except for the purpose of indicating that a vessel or a seaplane is in distress, and the use of any signals which may be confused with any of the above signals, is prohibited.**

ANNEX TO THE RULES

RECOMMENDATIONS ON THE USE OF RADAR INFORMATION AS AN AID TO AVOIDING COLLISIONS AT SEA

(1) Assumptions made on scanty information may be dangerous and should be avoided.

(2) **A vessel navigating with the aid of radar in restricted visibility must,** in compliance with Rule 16 (*a*), **go at a moderate speed.** Information obtained from the use of radar is one of the circumstances to be taken into account when determining

moderate speed. In this regard it must be recognised that small vessels, small icebergs and similar floating objects may not be detected by radar. **Radar indications of one or more vessels in the vicinity may mean that "moderate speed" should be slower than a mariner without radar might consider moderate in the circumstances.**

(3) **When navigating in restricted visibility the radar range and bearing alone do not constitute ascertainment of the position of the other vessel under Rule 16 (*b*) sufficiently to relieve a vessel of the duty to stop her engines and navigate with caution when a fog signal is heard forward of the beam.**

(4) When action has been taken under Rule 16 (*c*) to avoid a close quarters situation, it is essential to make sure that such action is having the desired effect. Alterations of course or speed or both are matters as to which the mariner must be guided by the circumstances of the case.

(5) Alterations of course alone may be the most effective action to avoid close quarters provided that:—

(*a*) There is sufficient sea room.

(*b*) It is made in good time.

(*c*) It is substantial. A succession of small alterations of course should be avoided.

(*d*) It does not result in a close quarters situation with other vessels.

(6) **The direction of an alteration of course is a matter in which the mariner must be guided by the circumstances of the case. An alteration to starboard, particularly when vessels are approaching apparently on opposite or nearly opposite courses, is generally preferable to an alteration to port.**

(7) An alteration of speed, either alone or in conjunction with an alteration of course, should be substantial. A number of small alterations of speed should be avoided.

(8) **If a close quarters situation is imminent, the prudent action may be to take all way off the vessel.**

Chapter Seven

Lifesaving

Much of the yachtsman's knowledge of life-saving equipment and general safety afloat is derived from the many excellent yachting publications, from yachting and sailing clubs and from advice given by more experienced hands.

There is, however, a wealth of information on the safety of life at sea published by both the Department of Trade and Industry and, the Hydrographic Office. The average yachtsman is too often blissfully unaware of much of this vital information. Certain yachts are required by law to comply with the provisions of various Statutory Instruments.

Too much emphasis cannot be placed on the need for constant vigilance where safety at sea is concerned. Help may be a long way off!

LIFE-SAVING APPLIANCES (L.S.A.)

The Merchant Shipping (Life-saving appliances) Rules, 1965 require pleasure yachts of 45 feet in length and over (Class XII ships) to carry certain safety equipment as follows. Length in this context is Registered Length.

(1) **Yachts of 70 feet in length and over must carry:**
    (*a*)   At least two liferafts having sufficient aggregate capacity to accommodate twice the number of persons on board. Each raft must be capable of being launched on either side of the yacht.
    (*b*)   At least four lifebuoys, two of which must have lifebuoy lights attached. At least two of the others, one on each side of the yacht, must have 15 fathoms of buoyant line attached.
    (*c*)   At least two smoke markers.
    Note These need not be attached to the buoys. They may be carried close to the buoys in such a manner as to be easily released. Smoke markers may be incorporated in the lifebuoy lights (Extract from M. Notice 496).
    (*d*)   At least one approved lifejacket for each person on board.
    (*e*)   At least six pyrotechnic distress signals of the rocket parachute signal type, or the red stars type.
    (*f*)   At least one line throwing appliance in a watertight case. This consists of four rockets, and four half-inch circumference lines of suitable length and having a breaking strain of not less than 250 pounds.

In yachts of 75 feet in length and over the minimum range of the rocket appliance must not be less than 250 yards. For yachts of less than 75 feet in length the range must not be less than 200 yards.

Note In addition to the above requirements, yachts of 85 feet in length and over must carry a lifeboat or Class C boat.

(2) **Yachts of less than 70 feet in length which proceed to sea a greater distance than three miles from the coast, or go to sea during the months of November to March shall carry:—**

(a)   At least one liferaft of sufficient aggregate capacity to accommodate all persons on board.
(b)   At least two lifebuoys, one of which must have a light attached.
(c)   At least one smoke float.
(d)   At least ten fathoms of buoyant line.
(e)   At least one lifejacket for each person on board.
(f)   At least six pyrotechnic distress signals as defined in 1 (e).

(3) **Yachts of less than 70 feet in length which do not go to sea, or which go to sea from April to October inclusive and not more than three miles from the coast, shall carry:—**

(a)   Lifebuoys equivalent to half the total number of persons carried, and not less than two. One lifebuoy must have a light attached.
(b)   At least one smoke marker.
(c)   At least one lifejacket for each person on board.
(d)   At least ten fathoms of buoyant line.
(e)   At least six pyrotechnic distress signals as defined in 1 (e).

(4) **Yachts of less than 70 feet in length which are confined to "smooth water areas" as defined in Schedule 1 of the L.S.A. Rules, shall carry:—**

(a)   At least two lifebuoys, one of which must have a light attached.
(b)   At least one smoke marker.
(c)   At least one lifejacket for each person on board.
(d)   At least ten fathoms of buoyant line.

Note All the above-mentioned equipment must be of a Department of Trade & Industry approved type. In the case of lifejackets they may conform with British Standard Specification No. BS 3595 : 1963. They must not depend solely on oral inflation.

REPLACEMENT OF PYROTECHNICS ETC.

Notice to Mariners No. 4 1971 states that line throwing rockets, distress rockets, and red hand flares etc. should be replaced after two years from the date of manufacture which is stamped on each rocket; rockets, etc. manufactured after the 1st September, 1971 should be replaced after three years.

Smoke markers should be treated similarly, but should be carefully inspected at frequent intervals and condemned if faulty.

MASTERS AND OWNERS SHOULD ENSURE THAT OBSOLETE ROCKETS ETC. ARE DISPOSED OF IN DEEP WATER AND ADEQUATELY WEIGHTED. Obsolete rockets must NOT be fired for practice purposes as deterioration may have rendered them dangerous.

CONTENTS OF INFLATABLE LIFERAFTS

When liferafts of an approved type are carried they shall contain the following items:

- (*a*)   One buoyant rescue quoit with 100 feet of buoyant line attached.
- (*b*)   One safety knife and one bailer for liferafts up to and including the 12 man capacity type.
  Two safety knives and two bailers for liferafts larger than the above.
- (*c*)   Two sponges.
- (*d*)   One sea anchor permanently attached to the raft.
- (*e*)   Two paddles.
- (*f*)   One puncture repair outfit.
- (*g*)   One pump or bellows.
- (*h*)   Two safety tin-openers.
- (*i*)   One first aid kit.
- (*j*)   One graduated rustproof cup.
- (*k*)   One waterproof torch suitable for sending morse, with a spare set of batteries and bulb.
- (*l*)   Two parachute distress rockets.
- (*m*)   Three hand-held flares.
- (*n*)   One pint of fresh water per person in sealed cans.
- (*o*)   Six anti-seasickness tablets per person.
- (*p*)   Instructions on how to survive in the raft.
- (*q*)   One copy of the Rescue Signal Table.

Note Always ensure that the liferaft painter is securely attached to the yacht. Liferafts are to be serviced at an approved servicing depot at intervals of not more than 12 months.

YACHTS UNDER 45 FEET IN LENGTH

A large number of pleasure yachts are considerably smaller than those mentioned in the L.S.A. Rules and, are not therefore legally required to comply with the Rules. Owners of such yachts should, however, be guided by the new requirements for yachts under 45 feet issued July 1971 by the Department of Trade and Industry. These are fully described in Reed's Nautical Almanac—Safety at Sea Section.

USE OF ROCKETS AND FLARES

The rocket parachute distress signals, and the red star signals should be of high candle power. Their main purpose is to summon help which may lie beyond the horizon. They should therefore be used sparingly and NOT fired one after another. When help is SEEN the red hand-held flares may be used to pin-point the yacht's position. Learn how to fire them before an emergency arises.

MAINTENANCE OF LIFE-SAVING EQUIPMENT

The Master or owner should ensure that all L.S.A. equipment is in good order and properly stowed. The crew should be made aware of the stowage and be able to use the equipment in an emergency. It is too late to start studying the instructions on a dark night with the yacht disintegrating about you!

Emergency procedures should be planned and practiced so that all hands know precisely what to do in an emergency.

It is the Master or owner's duty to ensure that the code of safety, whether statutory or private, is fully understood and complied with.

LIFEJACKETS

Where water is a hazard, aids to safety should never be ignored. It is just as easy to fall in, in estuaries and inland waters, as it is offshore or deep sea. A moment's carelessness in the necessary position and you will need to swim. If you are unconscious or have never learned to swim, and become exhausted through trying, you may not survive.

A lifejacket is designed to give correct support to just such a person provided it is donned correctly. The importance of correct donning cannot be emphasised too much and any supplier should be able to provide Donning Instructions with any lifejacket you may purchase. The instructions should be studied and practised.

Lifejackets approved by the Department of Trade & Industry may be filled with kapok or blocks of foam. They are made to two specifications, one for persons weighing 70 pounds or more and one for persons weighing less than 70 pounds. If donned according to instructions they will, in still water, turn the wearer to a safe floating position within five seconds of entering the water and give support to the head, keeping the mouth not less than six inches above water.

Ships of Class XII, i.e. Pleasure Yachts, may have lifejackets which comply with British Standard BS 3595 : 1963. A new edition of this standard was published in July 1969. However, the lifejacket chosen must be one that does not depend wholly upon oral inflation.

When sailing, lifejackets should be worn by all on board and when not in use they should be stowed carefully in an easily accessible place. They should be kept clear of damp and vermin, and aired occasionally when they may be given a thorough inspection for damage or deterioration.

INFLATABLE LIFERAFTS

An inflatable liferaft delivered to a yacht will be in a valise or sealed container according to your order. You will not see it or its contents until the operating cord is pulled, for interest, by accident, or in earnest when an emergency arises. This is a costly exercise as the raft must then be returned to a Service Station to be re-packed. This must be done in any case, for servicing, at twelve monthly intervals. Any Service Station will probably be pleased to show you an inflated raft and its contents. Ascertain your nearest one and ask. After a short visit your raft will be a stranger no longer.

When a liferaft is inflated, which takes place when the operating cord is pulled, it will be seen generally to be of an oval or round shape. Inflation is by carbon-dioxide gas carried in a cylinder attached to the underside of the raft. There are usually two buoyancy chambers. If one is punctured, the other will support the number of persons for which the raft is certificated. A highly visible cover arises automatically on inflation by means of inflated arches. There is a lamp powered by a sea-activated cell on top of the cover and also inside.

The two openings in the cover can be closed against the weather.

The floor is of double thickness and may be inflated by hand bellows to provide insulation against cold water.

There is a boarding ladder at each entrance.

The construction of the raft includes pockets under the floor to minimise drifting and two sea anchors are provided also. If the raft is inverted on inflation it can easily be righted by one person standing on the gas bottle and pulling on the straps fitted to the underside. It can also be towed.

There is a survival pack inside.

On entering a raft after abandoning ship the *initial* procedure might be as follows:

Seat survivors round the perimeter with feet towards the centre.

Dry inside, using sponges provided to mop up any water.

When all in, adjust canopy openings for protection as required.

Issue anti-sea sickness tablets and give first aid if and as necessary.

USE OF ROCKET APPARATUS AND BREECHES BUOY

There are visual signals laid down for use between the shore and ships in distress off, or stranded on, the coast of the United Kingdom. (See Fig. 7.1). Most Coastguard Rescue Companies and lifeboats include trained Signalmen and the signalling system laid down must be followed **STRICTLY**. Remember, however, that signal lamp or semaphore communication, if established, will be a great help.

Should lives be in danger and your vessel be in a position where rescue by the rocket rescue equipment is possible, a rocket with line attached will be fired from the shore across your vessel. Get hold of this line as soon as you can. When you have got hold of it, signal to the shore, as in Fig. 7.1.

Alternatively, should your vessel carry a line-throwing appliance and this is first used to fire a line ashore, this line will not be of sufficient strength to haul out the Whip and those on the shore will, therefore, secure it to a stouter line. When this is done, they will signal, as in Fig. 7.1. On seeing their signal, haul in the line which was fired from the vessel until the stouter line is on board.

It may happen that with a yacht, the state of the weather and her condition, e.g. dismasted, will not admit of a hawser being set up, in which case the Whip will be used without the hawser as described in the following routine.

When the rocket line is held, make the appropriate signal to the shore (Fig. 7.1) and proceed as follows:—

(1) When you see the appropriate signal. i.e. "haul away", made from the shore, haul upon the rocket line until you get a tail block with an endless fall rove through it (called the "Whip"). See Figs. 7.2 and 7.3.

(2) Make the tail block fast, close up to the mast or other convenient position, bearing in mind that the fall should be kept clear from chafing any part of the vessel, and that space must be left above the block for the hawser. Unbend the rocket line from the Whip. When the tail block is made fast and the rocket line unbent from the Whip, signal to the shore again, as in Fig. 7.1.

(3) As soon as this signal is seen on the shore a hawser will be bent to the Whip, and will be hauled off to the ship by those on shore. Except when there are rocks, piles or other obstructions between the ship and the shore, a bowline will have been made with the end of the hawser round the hauling part of the Whip.

SIGNALS TO BE EMPLOYED IN CONNECTION WITH THE USE OF SHORE LIFE SAVING APPARATUS

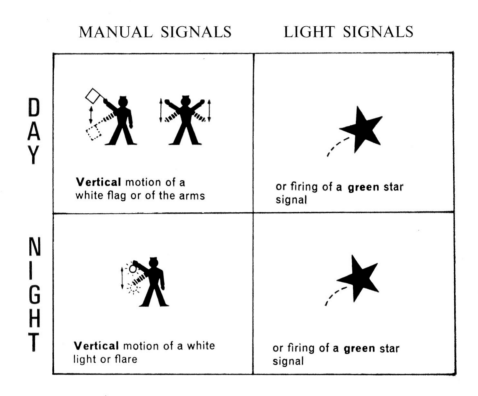

MANUAL SIGNALS   **LIGHT SIGNALS**

DAY

Vertical motion of a white flag or of the arms

or firing of a **green** star signal

NIGHT

Vertical motion of a white light or flare

or firing of a **green** star signal

MEANING

In general: Affirmative

Specifically: Rocket line is held
                    Tail block is made fast
                    Hawser is made fast
                    Man is in the breeches buoy
                    Haul away

Fig. 7.1

SIGNALS TO BE EMPLOYED IN CONNECTION WITH THE USE OF LIFE SAVING APPARATUS

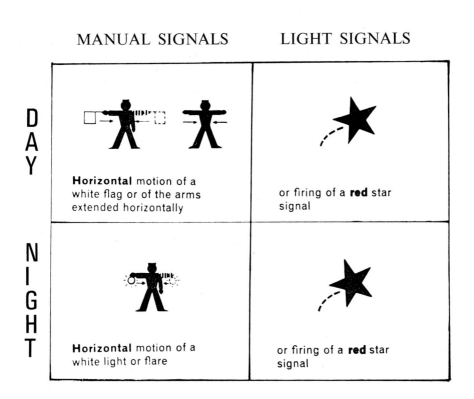

MANUAL SIGNALS   LIGHT SIGNALS

DAY

Horizontal motion of a white flag or of the arms extended horizontally

or firing of a **red** star signal

NIGHT

Horizontal motion of a white light or flare

or firing of a **red** star signal

MEANING

In general: Negative

Specifically: Slack away
Avast hauling

Fig. 7.1a

Using hawser and whip with the breeches buoy

Fig. 7.2

Using endless whip without the hawser and the small snatch block

Fig. 7.3

(4) When the hawser is got on board, the bowline should be cast off. Then, having seen that the end of the hawser is clear of the Whip, the end should be brought up between the two parts of the Whip and made fast to the same part of the ship as the tail block but just above it and with the tally board close up to the position to which the end of the hawser is secured (this will allow the breeches buoy to come right out and will facilitate entry to the buoy).

(5) When the hawser has been made fast on board, unbend the Whip from the hawser and see that the bight of the Whip has not been hitched to any part of the vessel and that it runs free in the block. Then signal to the shore, as in Fig. 7.1.

(6) The men on shore will then set the hawser taut, and by means of the Whip will haul off to the ship the breeches buoy into which the person to be hauled ashore is to get. He should sit well down in the breeches buoy and when he is secure, signal again to the shore, as in Fig. 7.1 and the men on shore will haul the person in the breeches buoy to the shore. When he is landed the empty breeches buoy will be hauled back to the ship. This operation will be repeated until all persons are landed.
During the course of these operations, should it be necessary to signal either from ship to shore or vice versa, to "Slack Away" or "Avast Hauling" this signal should be made in accordance with Fig. 7.1a.
A simplified diagram of the breeches buoy rigged between ship and shore is in Fig. 7.4.

ROCKET LIFE·SAVING APPARATUS

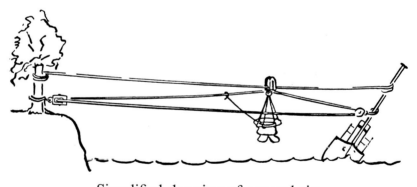

Simplified drawing of general rig

Fig. 7.4

LINE THROWING ROCKETS

If you have a Line Throwing Appliance it should consist of four rockets and four lines each of $\frac{1}{2}$ inch circumference and a breaking strain of not less than 250 pounds, together with cartridges to be placed in the gun or patent container in order to fire it. The rocket in this appliance must never be fired unless a line is attached to it. There should

REPLIES FROM LIFE·SAVING STATIONS OR MARITIME RESCUE UNITS TO DISTRESS SIGNALS MADE BY A SHIP OR PERSON

LIGHT SIGNALS   OTHER SIGNALS

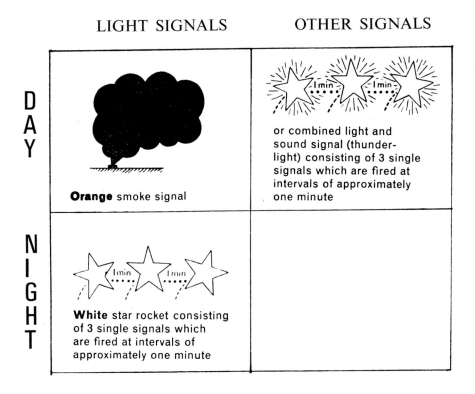

D A Y

Orange smoke signal

or combined light and sound signal (thunder-light) consisting of 3 single signals which are fired at intervals of approximately one minute

N I G H T

White star rocket consisting of 3 single signals which are fired at intervals of approximately one minute

MEANING

You are seen—
Assistance will be given as soon as possible
Repetition of such signal shall have the same meaning.

Fig. 7.5

also be an asbestos glove for use when firing and full instructions for use. These give an indication of the angle at which the appliance should be held and this will vary according to whether the shot is to be made with, against or across the wind.

The rockets have their date of filling stamped on them and should be renewed after three years if unused.

The whole appliance should be kept in a watertight case and be inspected regularly for deterioration.

LANDING SIGNALS FOR THE GUIDANCE OF SMALL BOATS WITH CREWS OR PERSONS IN DISTRESS

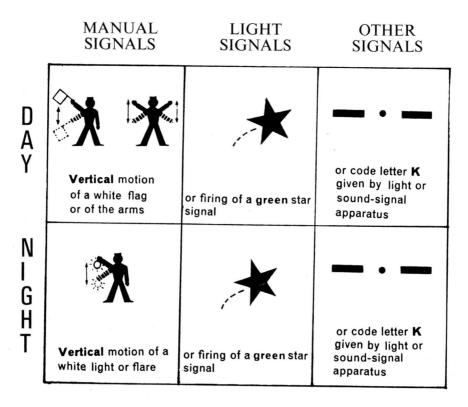

MANUAL SIGNALS	LIGHT SIGNALS	OTHER SIGNALS
DAY Vertical motion of a white flag or of the arms	or firing of a **green** star signal	or code letter **K** given by light or sound-signal apparatus
NIGHT Vertical motion of a white light or flare	or firing of a **green** star signal	or code letter **K** given by light or sound-signal apparatus

MEANING

This is the best place to land

Fig. 7.6

DISTRESS SIGNALS

The International Distress Signals are laid down in Rule 31 of the Regulations for Preventing Collisions at Sea. (See Chapter 6).

If you have provided yourself with rockets and flares don't panic in an emergency and set them all off at once. Use your high signals first, i.e. the parachute or star signals. These are designed to eject stars at a minimum height of 600 feet having a minimum luminosity of 15 000 candlepower.

LANDING SIGNALS FOR THE GUIDANCE OF SMALL BOATS WITH CREWS OR PERSONS IN DISTRESS

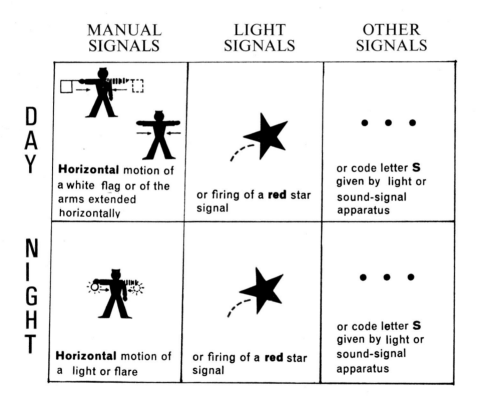

	MANUAL SIGNALS	LIGHT SIGNALS	OTHER SIGNALS
DAY	**Horizontal** motion of a white flag or of the arms extended horizontally	or firing of a **red** star signal	or code letter **S** given by light or sound-signal apparatus
NIGHT	**Horizontal** motion of a light or flare	or firing of a **red** star signal	or code letter **S** given by light or sound-signal apparatus

MEANING

Landing here highly dangerous

Fig. 7.6a

LANDING SIGNALS FOR THE GUIDANCE OF SMALL
BOATS WITH CREWS OR PERSONS IN DISTRESS

	MANUAL SIGNALS	LIGHT SIGNALS	OTHER SIGNALS
D A Y	 1 **Horizontal** motion of a white flag, followed by 2 the placing of the white flag in the ground and 3 by the carrying of another white flag in the direction to be indicated	1 or firing of a **red** star signal vertically and 2 a **white** star signal in the direction towards the better landing place	1 or signalling the code letter **S** (...) followed by the code letter **R** (.−.) if a better landing place for the craft in distress is located more to the *right* in the direction of approach 2 or signalling the code letter **S** (...) followed by the code letter **L** (.−..) if a better landing place for the craft in distress is located more to the *left* in the direction of approach
N I G H T	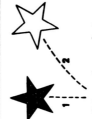 1 **Horizontal** motion of a white light or flare 2 followed by the placing of the white light or flare on the ground and 3 the carrying of another white light or flare in the direction to be indicated	1 or firing of a **red** star signal vertically and a 2 **white** star signal in the direction towards the better landing place	

**Landing here highly dangerous—a more favourable location for
landing is in the direction indicated**

Fig. 7.6b

Remember that though the Coastguard may see your first rocket, some time may elapse before rescue vessels reach you. If, by that time, you have used all your signals the rescuers may have a difficult task to pinpoint you in rough weather.

Keep your hand flares until you can see rescue craft in your vicinity.

When shore lifesaving stations, or maritime rescue units receive distress signals made by a ship they make replies as indicated in Fig. 7.5.

The use of any of the International Distress Signals or any others which may be confused with them is prohibited except for the purpose of indicating that a vessel is in distress.

If these signals are used, except for indicating distress, the user may be fined up to £50 and be liable in addition to pay compensation for any labour undertaken, risk incurred or loss sustained as a result.

LANDING SIGNALS

These are signals used by Coastguards on the shore for the guidance of small boats, with crews or persons in distress, which are approaching the coast. See Figs 7.6, 7.6*a* and 7.6*b*.

SAFETY AND URGENCY SIGNALS

Urgency Signals are used in Wireless Telegraphy (W/T) and Radio Telephony (R/T) when the calling station has a very urgent message to transmit concerning the safety of a ship, aircraft, other vehicle or person.

They are not Distress Signals. In **W/T** procedure an Urgency Signal is prefixed **"XXX"** and in **R/T** precedure the word **PAN** precedes the message.

Safety Signals indicate that a station is about to transmit a message concerning the safety of navigation or give an important meteorological warning. In **W/T** procedure they are prefixed **"TTT"** and in **R/T** procedure the word **SÉCURITÉ** precedes the message.

PILOT SIGNALS

There is only one signal which may be used to indicate that a vessel requires a Pilot. It is the single-letter signal **G.**

In restricted visibility, whether by day or night, the signal may be made by any method laid down in the International Code of Signals 1969 (See Chapter 10) except Flag signalling, flashing light signalling or signalling by hand flags or arms.

In unrestricted visibility:

By Day, any of the methods may be used.

By Night, any of the methods except flag signalling, hand flags or arms, may be used. If this Signal is used or displayed for any purpose other than that of summoning a Pilot the user is liable to a fine of up to £20.

Chapter Eight

Fire

Fire is a frightening prospect at the best of times, wherever it breaks out and no matter how small it appears to be, but it is generally accepted that a fire afloat is the worst fire of all unless it is dealt with quickly and properly in the initial stages. Ashore, it is possible to summon the nearest Fire Brigade if an outbreak cannot be extinguished by first-aid fire fighting equipment; afloat, however—particularly if some distance from shore or even the nearest boat—immediate assistance is out of the question, so the outbreak must be put out quickly by equipment available with the correct extinguishing medium; this is most important.

Fire consists of three ingredients: combustible material, heat and oxygen. Fire-fighting consists of removing one or more of these items, namely removing the combustible material, the cooling of such material and the air surrounding it to below ignition point and excluding the oxygen by blanketing the fire or shutting off the ventilation.
If fire occurs while at sea stop the ship or manoeuvre so the wind blows the fire over-board by the shortest route. If necessary, go astern. If in port and the fire is beyond your control, call local Fire Brigade.

FIRE EXTINGUISHING MEDIA

One of the old sea-shanties lustily enjoins mariners to "fetch a bucket of water, boys" for the fires "in the galley" and "down below"; whereas water was the only known remedy for outbreaks in those bygone days, fire safety for marine craft of today requires something more than the melodic bucket! For example, inboard engines with their accompanying fuel tanks and the Butane and Calor gas used now for cooking and heating are major fire risks in modern cruising yachts or power boats and, water is certainly not suitable for extinguishing fires involving highly flammable fuels and gases. Water, of course, is the commonest extinguishing medium, but over the years new technologies have introduced corresponding fire risks and today there are other extinguishing media developed to combat these specialised risks, including foam, carbon dioxide (CO_2), dry powder and vaporising liquids.

The Table below shows on what types of fire risk each medium is suitable.

Types of Fire	Suitable Fire Extinguishing Media
Wood, cloth, paper or similar combustible materials.	Water
Flammable liquids—petrols, oils, greases, fats, etc.	Foam; Carbon Dioxide (CO_2); Dry Powder; Vaporising Liquids.
Electrical—i.e fire outbreaks involving "live" equipment.	Carbon Dioxide (CO_2); Dry Powder; Vaporising Liquids.
Butane and other gases	Dry Powder

Water should never be used on flammable or electrical fires.
Foam must not be used on electrical outbreaks.
A "general-purpose" type Dry Powder can also be used for fires involving combustible materials (wood, cloth, etc.)

Once it is generally appreciated what should and should not be used, it is relatively simple to check all the possible fire risks aboard and ensure that the appropriate safety equipment is adequately provided.

FIRE PROTECTION EQUIPMENT

Safety regulations lay down minimum requirements of fire extinguishing equipment for various sizes of boats, of course, and when installing fire fighting equipment the prime consideration should be its reliability; it is strongly advisable that this should not only conform to British Standard Specifications but also be approved by the Fire Offices' Committee and/or the Department of Trade and Industry. In this respect there is no dearth of expertise available for assistance.

HAND FIRE EXTINGUISHERS

Hand fire extinguishers play a vital role since they enable that all-important action to be taken on the spot during the first few seconds of a fire outbreak. Extinguishers charged with any of the above-mentioned media are provided in a variety of sizes:

Dry Powder

The general-purpose type dry powder is the new fire extinguishing medium which is effective against fires of all classes—electrical, flammable and combustible materials. Its action on any fire is remarkably speedy and effective, yet it is unaffected by extremes of temperature, does not deteriorate and is non-conductive and non-toxic. Hand extinguishers charged with this dry powder are therefore ideal for dealing with composite fire hazards such as those commonly encountered in boats, where wood, cloth, *etc.* will often be involved in an outbreak with electrical gear or petrol and oil.

Stored pressure type extinguishers, pressurised by nitrogen or dry air, are provided with capacities of 5 lb. (Fig. 8.1), 10 lb. and 20 lb. of general-purpose dry powder. Each extinguisher is fitted with a pressure gauge and is easily operated by a controllable discharge lever. The 10 lb. and 20 lb. models are fitted with flexible discharge hoses.

Foam

For fighting fires involving oils and spirits, foam spreads quickly over the surface of the blazing liquid in the form of a "blanket", thus smothering the fire and providing a seal against re-ignition. The mechanical foam extinguisher (Fig. 8.2), of 2 gallons capacity is activated simply by striking the knob in the operating head and spreading the resultant foam jet over the blazing surface with the flexible hose and branchpipe.

Fig. 8.1   General Purpose Dry Powder Extinguisher. Suitable for outbreaks involving combustible, flammable and electrical materials

Fig. 8.2   Foam Extinguisher for flammable liquid fires

Fig. 8.3   Water Extinguisher (gas pressure) for outbreaks involving combustibles—wood, cloth, etc.

Water

This medium is recommended for fires involving combustible materials (wood, cloth, etc. and the extinguisher illustrated (Fig. 8.3), is filled with 2 gallons of water and a CO_2 gas cartridge provides the necessary pressure to expel the contents. It is operated simply by striking the plunger in the top cap.

Carbon Dioxide

CO_2 gas is highly effective in smothering fire quickly, cleanly and safely; it is non-injurious, non-toxic, non-conductive and non-corrosive. It is particularly recommended for use against any type of fire outbreak in enclosed areas including highly flammable or electrical fires. Carbon Dioxide extinguishers are provided in three sizes, containing $2\frac{1}{2}$ lb., 5 lb. (Fig. 8.4) and 10 lb. of liquified CO_2 gas respectively. Each model is fitted with a "thumb-push" valve by which the gas can be discharged or halted at will. The $2\frac{1}{2}$ lb. and 5 lb. models embody a rotating, non-conductive distributor horn and, the 10 lb. model is fitted with a length of flexible high-pressure hose and discharge horn.

Vaporising Liquids:

BCF (Bromochlorodifluoromethane) is a powerful new fire extinguishing medium which kills fires of the intense flammable category with an instantaneous smothering action, yet the vapour is clinically clean and leaves no trace; it is also safe to use on electrical outbreaks. Stored pressure type extinguishers are provided with capacities of 3 lb., 8 lb. (Fig. 8.5) and 16 lb. of BCF and, like the dry powder models, each extinguisher is easily operated by a squeeze-grip lever.

Each in their own way, therefore, the above extinguishers are suitable for *incipient* fire outbreaks—i.e. fighting fires in their initial stages. However, we referred earlier to the primary fire risk areas in modern cruising yachts—the engine and fuel tank compartments. An added advantage is to protect these areas with a built in-fire extinguishing installation which will provide an almost instantaneous "knock out" the moment a fire outbreak occurs. With the primary fire risk areas protected by "remote control", as it were, physical fire fighting may only be necessary for possible outbreaks incidental to the main fire or for dealing with incipient outbreaks in the residential quarters of the boat.

Left:

Fig. 8.4 Carbon Dioxide (CO_2) Extinguisher for flammable and electrical fires.

Right:

Fig. 8.5 Vaporizing Liquid—"B.C.F."—the new and powerful medium for flammable and electrical fires.

Fig. 8.6

BCF Fire Extinguishing Installation. By depressing the lever B.C.F. is discharged into the protected areas. The extinguisher can also be removed from the bracket and used as a portable appliance.

FIRE EXTINGUISHING INSTALLATIONS
BCF System

This system comprises one or more pairs of BCF extinguishers manifolded together and fitted outside the fire risk area (in a cockpit locker or similar location). From the manifold a feed pipe leads to a system of perforated pipes arranged to spray the entire area.

The extinguishers are each charged with 10 lb. of BCF and are operated individually either by a manual pull-handle control or by an electrical push-button switch; the pull-handle method has the advantage of being independent of electricity supply. The operating mechanism releases the BCF under pressure through the spray pipes and discharge of this potent medium is effected into the protected space. The operating controls are arranged to discharge one extinguisher only at a time; normally the contents of the single container will completely smother the fire. The twin container is fitted into the system as a reserve available for use on any subsequent fire outbreak occurring before the expended extinguisher has been replaced.

Another BCF fire fighting system has been developed to meet the need for a small, lightweight and reasonably priced installation. It comprises a BCF extinguisher fitted into a special bracket situated outside the fire risk area. The outlet of the extinguisher fits through an aperture in the top of the bracket which is connected to a small-bore distribution pipe with discharge nozzles installed in the protected compartments. The extinguisher is operated by depressing the release lever which releases the

BCF into the protected area. If necessary, it is easily removed from the bracket and can be used as a portable appliance in any other part of the boat.

Two such systems are provided incorporating either a 3 lb. or 8 lb. BCF extinguisher the 3 lb. model (Fig. 8.6) protects an area up to 60 cu. ft. and the 8 lb. model protects up to 160 cu. ft.

Carbon Dioxide System:

As already mentioned, Carbon Dioxide is particularly recommended for fire outbreaks in enclosed areas and a CO_2 installation is another fire extinguishing system suitable for engine and fuel tank protection.

Fig. 8.7 shows a typical fixed installation designed to provide complete fire protection for the engine, fuel tanks and other fire danger points of a motor cruiser, but this type of built-in system is easily adapted for all designs of motor driven craft.

It consists of a CO_2 gas cylinder, fitted with a lever-type piercing head remotely operated by cable and connected by pipeline to suitably placed discharge nozzles. In case of fire, the pull-handle is operated and all the protected spaces are instantly flooded with CO_2 gas.

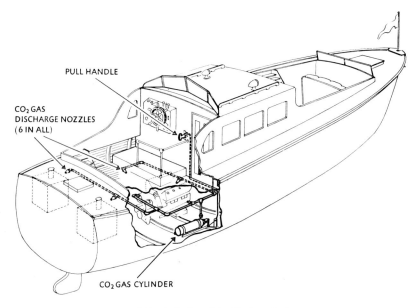

PULL HANDLE

CO_2 GAS
DISCHARGE NOZZLES
(6 IN ALL)

CO_2 GAS CYLINDER

Fig. 8.7   A Carbon Dioxide Installation.

THE HUMAN ELEMENT

Having now established all the possible fire risks aboard and ensured that the appropriate safety equipment is installed, there is one more thing which must be taken into account—human nature.

No matter how much equipment is provided the success of any fire fighting operations can be measured only by a complete understanding on the part of *everyone* aboard of the prevalent fire risks and of the most efficient ways to tackle them.

After all, although the owner has complied with regulations and himself may be well versed with the equipment installed, *other* people aboard may not be so conversant. It is advisable, therefore, to acquaint everyone with the location of the equipment and the method of operation, as where fire is concerned it is obviously far better to be forewarned and prepared than, ultimately, ignorant and useless.

It cannot be emphasised enough that everyone aboard should know exactly what to do in a fire emergency: (1) recognise the type of fire it is (combustible, flammable or electrical); (2) know where to find the appropriate equipment and, (3) know how to use it.

It is surprising how many people in general know so little (or even care) about fire safety; "it always happens to the other chap" is a very short-sighted attitude which could so easily end up, one day, with needless and tragic consequences.

SAFETY PRECAUTIONS

REFUELLING PETROL TANKS

Use only the approved safety can equipped with a flexible hose spout or in the case of a portable tank disconnect and fill ashore.

Prevent petrol overspilling into bilges—should liquid escape in a confined space the vapour when mixed with air becomes a dangerous source of fire or explosion.

It is preferable not to use petrol below deck and not for cooking where naked flame would be a constant source of danger.

Petrol tanks should be stowed well away from the engine, larger tanks fitted with a ventilation pipe.

After filling tanks allow a period of some minutes to elapse in order to clear the vapour before starting the engine.

Fuel tanks should never be filled to overflowing but a space left for expansion.

Avoid refuelling at night.

No smoking to be allowed when refuelling.

Stop engines, light sets, cooking stoves, etc. when refuelling and close all openings, port holes and hatches.

SMOKING

Do not smoke in bunks or leave lighted cigarettes unattended.

CLEANING MATERIALS

If these are contaminated with oil or other combustible substances dispose of them immediately or stow in sealed containers.

FIRE APPLIANCES

Maintain a regular inspection and recharge at appropriate times.

GALLEY

Keep clean and do not leave unattended when fuel is switched on.
Turn off gas at source after use.

BUTANE GAS

Stow containers in open where possible with drain leading overboard.
Refrain from using hose connections or rubber piping.
Keep a regular check on all fuel line piping and joints.
Make sure gas cannot escape into the bilges—being heavier than air it always sinks to the lowest point and remains there for a considerable time as a constant explosion risk.
Turn off gas at source after use.
Make sure all electrical wiring is in good order. Avoid sparks from short circuits.
Use only safety torches in confined spaces.

LOCKERS

Inspect regularly and keep free of oily clothes and combustible material.

BILGES

Keep oil out of bilges and clean up any spills immediately.
Keep clean and well-ventilated.
Keep pumped out regularly to extract any gas that may have accumulated.

GIVE THOUGHT TO WHAT WOULD HAPPEN IF A FIRE OCCURRED ON YOUR VESSEL AND REMEMBER THAT YOU ARE RESPONSIBLE FOR EVERY CREW MEMBER OR GUEST ON BOARD, MAN, WOMAN OR CHILD. SO BE PREPARED AND ARRANGE IN ADVANCE A PLAN OF OPERATION SHOULD FIRE OCCUR.

Chapter Nine

Merchant Shipping Notices
and
Admiralty Notices to Mariners

M. Notices are issued by the Marine Division of the Department of Trade and Industry; they contain information and rules or guidance on various matters of interest to the mariner. Many of these notices are concerned with the safety of life at sea and some are of particular interest to yachtsmen and the owners of other small craft.
It is impracticable within the scope of this book to deal with all the M. Notices appertaining to small craft. The yachtsman should therefore endeavour to obtain the relevant notices, possibly through the officers of his yacht club.

A brief summary of the more important M. Notices follows:—

Compass. Magnetic material should not be placed within ten feet of a standard compass or within five feet of a steering compass. The mariner is cautioned regarding the effect of moveable steel fittings and electrical equipment on the compass deviations, and the effect "laying-up" has on permanent magnetism, especially in small boats, (see also Chapter 15 of "Coastal Navigation", Reed's Yacht Master Series).

M.526. Bilge pumping systems should be in good order and used promptly in an emergency. The use of a flexible emergency hose is recommended in the event of bilge lines becoming blocked.

Note   This latter recommendation might apply to larger yachts, but as a general rule bilges are usually kept quite clean on yachts, so there is probably not so much danger of blocked lines.

Fire precautions. A petrol engine situated below deck should be in a separate well ventilated compartment, protected by fire resistant material and steel sheeting.
In an open launch a petrol engine should be situated aft and contained within watertight bulkheads to prevent the spread of petrol. The tank should be large enough to obviate the need for spare cans of fuel. Spilling arrangements should be incorporated to prevent petrol leaking to the bilges. Inlets and outlets should be protected with wire gauze diaphragms. Joints should be oil tight, soft solder should not be used. Carburettors should be in good order to prevent back-firing. Exhaust pipes should be cooled, and extinguishers ready at hand. It is further recommended that since petrol is so dangerous such engines should be adapted to run on paraffin.

The mariner is cautioned on the dangers of spontaneous combustion due to oil soaked rags and woodwork. Cleanliness should be practiced at all times in this respect.

M. 577. Use of Liquified Petroleum Gas (L.P.G.) in Domestic Installations and Appliances on Ships, Barges, Launches and Pleasure Craft.
Serious fires and explosions have occurred on pleasure craft due to leakage of L.P.G. In this notice the Department of Trade & Industry draws attention to these dangers and makes the following recommendations.

(1) Installations should comply at least with the British Standard Code of Practice C.P.399, Part 3 (1956). Individual appliances and fittings should comply with the relevant British Standard Specifications.

(2) The use of open flame appliances should be avoided. If installed however they should be well secured and a type where the flame is isolated, with air supply and combustion outlet piped to the open air. There is a danger of asphyxiation from gas leakage in enclosed spaces, adequate ventilation is most important. The following warning in red letters should be displayed alongside the appliance.

WARNING

BEFORE LIGHTING CHECK FOR LEAKS BUT NEVER WITH A NAKED FLAME. LACK OF VENTILATION CAN PROVE FATAL.

(3) Expert advice should be obtained before installing. Adequate maintenance should be provided whilst the appliance is in service.

(4) L.P.G. containers should be stowed on deck or in a well ventilated compartment on deck, so sited that leaking gas will disperse rapidly overboard. Containers should be well secured to prevent movement. Non-return valves should be incorporated close to the stop valve. Containers should never be lifted by means of a rope around the valve.

(5) Automatic safety gas cut-off devices should be incorporated in the supply line to each appliance.

(6) Compartments containing L.P.G. appliances should be well ventilated. Exhaust vents should be situated low in the compartment. Ventilation may be provided by self trimming cowls or rotating exhauster heads, but should be sited so that unshielded flames cannot be extinguished.

(7) A suitably sited automatic detection and alarm system should be provided.

(8) Action to be taken in the event of an alarm should be displayed on a notice and include the following:—
    (a) the need for constant alertness regarding leakage
    (b) the shutting-off of all L.P.G. appliances at the main, the stopping of smoking, the banning of naked lights for detecting leaks.
    (c) the use and maintenance of fire fighting appliances.

The yachtsman is urged to obtain a copy of this particular notice, as the above details are but a brief extract.

M.575. Heating Appliances burning solid fuel.
This notice draws attention to the dangers of asphyxiation from oxygen consuming devices, and the need for adequate ventilation especially in sleeping accommodation.

M.310. Draws the mariners' attention to the dangers involved in failing to **use appropriate fog signals.**

M.412. Use of wave quelling oils in rescue operations.
Experience has shown that vegetable, animal and fish oils are most suitable for quelling waves. Lubricating oils are useful, but heavy fuel oil should be used with caution when survivors are in the water.

M.396. Deals with dangers involved in **bathing in dock water.**

M.437. The attention of Masters and owners is drawn towards the necessity of **obtaining the latest navigational information.**

M.447. Misuse of Inflatable Liferafts.
When life-saving appliances are carried in compliance with a Statutory Instrument it is an offence to render them unfit for service.

M.480. Calcium Carbide Lifebuoy Light Signals.
The notice draws attention to the deterioration of chemicals and corrosive action on seams, and emphasises the need for periodic examination of such signals.

M.518. The second masthead light is required to be carried by vessels of 150 feet in length and over when towing or pushing another vessel.

M.535 Deals with **precautions when siting Radar in Merchant Ships.**
Yachtsmen would be advised to obtain a copy of this notice if they have radar, or intend installing it on their yacht.

M.537. Draws attention to the use of the identification signal for a pilot vessel, vis. four short blasts in succession.

M.551. Draws attention to the risks involved in **crossing drift nets,** i.e. damage to nets and the possibility of their fouling the propeller.

M.554. Concerns **radiotelephone distress procedure** and gives details of the three cards to be displayed in full view of the operating position.
     Card 1 deals with the transmitting procedure
     Card 2 deals with the reception of safety messages
         "MAYDAY" indicates DISTRESS
         "PAN" indicates URGENCY
         SECURITE indicates SAFETY
     Card 3 gives details of various procedures and the phonetic alphabet.
     Note. Full details of the above cards may be found in the International Code of
         Signals 1969 pp. xiv, xv.

M.572. Draws attention to the **effect of radio and other equipment on the magnetic compass.**

Vessels navigated stern foremost by means of a bow rudder carry two black balls in a horizontal line.

M.596 Yacht Master Certificates

Copies of this notice may be obtained gratis from any of the Department of Trade and Industry offices.

Candidates for the Department of Trade & Industry Yacht Master Certificate examination are advised to obtain copies of these notices so that the contents may be studied in greater depth.

Submarine Cables. Mariners are cautioned against anchoring in the vicinity of submarine cables. For damaging a submarine cable through culpable negligence the penalty may be imprisonment or a fine or both.

If a cable is fouled and cannot be slipped by normal methods the anchor and cable should be slipped. On no account should the cable be cut due to the serious risk of electric shock. Compensation may be claimed from the owner of the cable for sacrificed gear; the Master should make a declaration on form S10 within 24 hours of arrival at the Custom House or Coastguard etc. (See also N. to M. No. 12).

Lightvessels. Mariners are cautioned against navigating too close to Lightvessels. Attention is drawn to the danger involved in homing on a Lightvessel's radio beacon in the hope that her fog signal will be heard in ample time. Risk of collision can be avoided by ensuring that the radio bearing does not remain constant.

It must be emphasised that the above extracts from the various M. Notices are very brief. For more information the relevant M. Notice should be consulted.

ADMIRALTY NOTICES TO MARINERS (See also "Coastal Navigation").

Weekly Notices to Mariners are published by the Hydrographic office and are concerned mainly with the promulgation of navigational information.

At the beginning of each year the Annual Summary of Admiralty Notices to Mariners is published. This contains Annual Notices Nos. 1 to 22 (notices of a permanent nature), Temporary and Preliminary Notices, and Notices affecting Sailing Directions.

Candidates for the Yacht Master examination are advised to obtain a copy of the Annual Summary for the current year from their chart Agents.

The following is a brief summary of some of the Annual Notices of a permanent nature.

Notice No. 1. UNITED KINGDOM—DEFENDED PORTS MOVEMENT. CONTROL SIGNALS AND PORT EXAMINATION SERVICE. CLOSING OF PORTS, AND STOPPING OF MOVEMENT IN PORTS.

Signals displayed near the approaches to a port under control of the Ministry of Defence.

(*a*) Three red balls by day or three flashing red lights by night disposed vertically indicate "Entrance prohibited".

(*b*) Three green lights disposed vertically indicate "Entrance permitted".

(*c*) A blue flag by day or two red lights separated by a green light disposed vertically by night indicates "Movement of shipping within the port or anchorage prohibited".

If these signals are carried on the Examination vessel they will be in addition to her normal navigation lights.

Vessels are cautioned not to approach the entrance to a Controlled Port or enter a Dangerous area without permission, and are advised to communicate with any Patrol vessel in the offing.

THE EXAMINATION SERVICE

Where it is necessary to examine or establish the identity of vessels entering a port, this will be carried out by the Examination Service. Examination vessels fly the Blue Ensign (occasionally the White Ensign) and a special flag having a white over red rectangle with a blue surround.

If ordered to an Examination Anchorage it is forbidden to:—

(*a*) lower a boat.

(*b*) communicate with the shore or other ships.

(*c*) move the ship.

(*d*) work cables.

(*e*) allow anyone or anything to leave the ship.

Notice No. 4. DISTRESS AND RESCUE AT SEA

Much of the information contained in this notice is incorporated in the various parts of this book dealing with distress and rescue. The following section however is of particular interest to yachtsmen and is given in greater detail.

VISUAL SIGNALS USED BETWEEN SHORE STATIONS IN THE U.K. AND SHIPS IN DISTRESS.

In the event of a ship being in distress on the coast of the U.K. the following signals should be used in communications between the ship and the shore.

(*a*) REPLIES FROM LIFE-SAVING STATIONS OR RESCUE UNITS TO SHIPS DISTRESS SIGNALS

BY DAY —Orange smoke or combined light and sound signal (thunder light) consisting of three single signals fired at one minute intervals.

BY NIGHT—White star rocket consisting of three single signals fired at one minute intervals.

MEANING—You are seen—assistance will be given as soon as possible.

(*b*) LANDING SIGNALS FOR THE GUIDANCE OF SMALL BOATS WITH PEOPLE IN DISTRESS.

SIGNAL —Vertical motion of a white flag or arms by day, or vertical motion of a white light by night, or the firing of a green star-signal, or signalling Morse code letter K (— · —).

MEANING—This is the best place to land.

NOTE. A leading line may be indicated by the placing of a white light or flare low down and in line with the observer.

SIGNAL   —Horizontal motion of a white flag, or arms extended horizontally by day, or a horizontal motion of a white light by night, or the firing of a red star-signal, or the signalling of Morse code letter S ($\cdot \cdot \cdot$).

MEANING—Landing here is highly dangerous.

SIGNAL   —Horizontal motion of a white flag (by day), or a white light (by night), followed by placing the flag or light on the ground and walking in the direction of the safer landing place with another white flag or light. Firing a red star-signal vertically and a white star-signal in the direction of the safer landing place. The Morse code letter S ($\cdot \cdot \cdot$) followed by R ($\cdot - \cdot$) if a safer landing place is located to the right of the line of approach, or followed by L ($\cdot - \cdot\cdot$) if the safer landing lies to the left of the line of approach.

MEANING—Landing here is highly dangerous. A more favourable location lies in the direction indicated.

(*c*) SIGNALS TO BE EMPLOYED IN CONNECTION WITH THE USE OF SHORE BASED LIFE-SAVING APPARATUS, i.e. THE BREECHES BUOY.

SIGNAL   —Vertical motion of a white flag or arms (by day) or white light (by night), or firing a green star-signal.

MEANING—In general:—   "Affirmative".
          In particular:—"Rocket line is held".
                         "Tail block is made fast".
                         "Hawser is made fast".
                         "Man is in the Breeches Buoy".
                         "Haul away".

SIGNAL   —Horizontal motion of a white flag (by day) or a white light (by night), or arms extended horizontally, or firing a red star-signal.

MEANING—In general:—   "Negative".
          In particular:—"Slack away".
                         "Avast hauling".

(*d*) SIGNALS USED TO WARN A VESSEL SEEN TO BE STANDING INTO DANGER.

SIGNAL   —International Code Flags U or NF, or the Morse code letter U ($\cdot \cdot -$) sent by lamp, foghorn or whistle.

MEANING—You are running into danger.

NOTE. Attention may be called to these signals by a white flare, or a white star-rocket, or an explosive sound signal.

PROCEDURE USED IN RESCUE OPERATIONS INVOLVING THE BREECHES BUOY (See (*c*) above for appropriate signals).

If rescue by breeches buoy is possible a rocket line will be fired across the vessel in distress. The line should be held as soon as possible and the fact signalled to the shore.

The following procedure then takes place. See Figs. 7.1, 7.1A, 7.2, 7.3, 7.4.

(1) On receiving the "haul away" signal from the shore a tail block with an endless whip rove through it is hauled out on the rocket line by the distressed crew.

(2) The tail block is made fast close-up to a secure point on the yacht (mast etc.) and the rocket line unbent. Beware of any obstructions which may cause chafe. Signal to the shore "Tail block made fast".

(3) On receiving this signal the shore party will bend a hawser to the whip and haul it off to the distressed vessel. When conditions permit a bowline is made in the end of the hawser around the hauling part of the whip.

(4) When the hawser reaches the vessel it is cast off and made fast just above the tail block so that the talley board is close up to the securing point (mast etc.).

NOTE. It is important that the hawser is brought up between the two parts of the whip when casting off.

(5) When the hawser is secure, and the whip is checked to ensure that it runs free, signal to the shore "Hawser made fast".

(6) The shore party will now set the hawser taut and then haul off the breeches buoy to the vessel by means of the whip.

The rescued person should sit low down in the breeches buoy and when ready to be hauled off signal the fact to the shore party. The person will be hauled ashore and the procedure repeated until the rescue is complete.

NOTE. It is sometimes advisable not to use the hawser, in which case the breeches buoy will be operated on the whip only.

Notice No. 5 FIRING PRACTICE AND EXERCISE AREAS.

In view of the responsibility of range authorities to avoid accidents, practice areas will not normally be shown on charts. Range buoys, beacons, lights and targets which might pose a hazard to navigation will be shown.

(1) Craft operating as control vessels will display a red flag at the masthead.

(2) Remote-controlled craft are 68 feet in length and carry not under command lights and shapes in addition to normal navigation lights.

(3) Should a vessel find herself within an area being used for practice she should maintain her course and speed, but if prevented from so doing by the exigencies of navigation she should clear the area as soon as possible.

Notice No. 6. SEISMIC SURVEYS

Vessels engaged in seismic surveys carry the signals prescribed in Rule 4 (*c*) of the Regulations for Preventing Collisions at Sea. They may also fly the International Code flags PO and IR. Such vessels when firing charges may fly code flag B, by day, and show an all round red light at night. Mariners should give these vessels a very wide berth.

Notice No. 7. CAUTION WITH REGARD TO SHIPS APPROACHING FORMA-TIONS, CONVOYS, AIRCRAFT CARRIERS AND OTHER WARSHIPS.

Single vessels should take early action to keep clear of convoys and formations. Mariners are warned of the uncertainty of movements of aircraft carriers, and the fact that their steaming lights are placed off the centre line, with reduced horizontal separation. Their side lights may be carried on either side of the bridge so that the port side light may be 100 feet from the port side of the ship. Certain aircraft carriers carry four anchor lights below the flight deck. Two white lights are carried on the same plane not more than five feet below the flight deck at the fore end, and two similar lights are carried at least 15 feet below the forward lights at the after end.

Ships when minehunting display the signals prescribed in Rule 4 (c) and (e) of the Regulations for Preventing Collisions at Sea. Small boats and dinghies with divers may be operating in conjunction with these vessels. These small craft will show by night two all round red lights in a horizontal line six feet apart in addition to the lights required by Rule 7 of the Regulations for Preventing Collisions at Sea. Such vessels should be given a wide berth.

Notice No. 8. INFORMATION CONCERNING SUBMARINES.

(1) WARNING SIGNALS. British vessels fly the International Code group NEZ to indicate the presence of submerged submarines exercising in the vicinity. Mariners are cautioned to keep a sharp lookout for periscopes and snorts, and to give these vessels a wide berth.

SIGNALS FROM SUBMERGED SUBMARINES

White smoke candle with flame
Yellow smoke candles   } Used to indicate position upon request
Yellow and green pyro flares

Red pyro flares which may be accompanied by smoke candles } Keep clear. I am carrying out emergency surfacing procedure. Do NOT stop propellers. Clear the area immediately and stand by to render assistance.

Two yellow pyro flares or two white smoke candles at three minute intervals } Keep clear. I am preparing to surface. Do NOT stop propellers. Clear the immediate vicinity.

NOTE. Submarines are not always escorted by a surface vessel.

(2) NAVIGATION LIGHTS. The mariners attention is drawn to the unusual appearance of submarine lights which may give the impression of a much smaller vessel. Some submarines are fitted with a quick flashing (90 flashes per minute) amber light six feet above the aft steaming light.

NOTE. Do not confuse with the amber flashing light carried by hovercraft which flashes at the rate of 60 flashes per minute.

(3) SUNKEN SUBMARINE. A sunken submarine unable to surface may indicate her position as follows:—
(a) By releasing an indicator buoy
(b) By firing candles giving off yellow or white smoke.
(c) Pumping out oil.
(d) Blowing out air.

British submarines are equipped with two indicator buoys, one forward and one aft, labelled as such. The sighting of a subsunk buoy should be reported immediately, along with the serial number found below the word FORWARD or AFT.

If the buoy is sighted in depths exceeding 100 fathoms it is likely to be adrift. The mooring wire is half inch galvanised steel wire of breaking strain one ton. Its weight in water is 4·3 pounds per 100 feet length. Thus if no other means is available of checking whether the buoy is adrift (e.g. flow of tidal stream) a boat may be lowered and the wire weighed by hand. Very great care should be exercised in this operation as IT IS ABSOLUTELY VITAL NOT TO PART THE WIRE. On no account should the boat be secured to the wire.

Survivors arriving at the surface are likely to be exhausted, a small boat is therefore desirable if circumstances permit. Larger ships (and yachts) should stand clear of the immediate area. The presence of help may be indicated to the submariners by running the echo sounder or banging on the hull below the waterline at frequent intervals.

THE SUBSUNK BUOY is cylindrical, 2 feet 3 inches in diameter and $18\frac{1}{2}$ inches deep, floating with a freeboard of 6 inches. It is painted in International orange and carries a whip aerial, a flashing light and "cats-eye" reflectors. Each buoy carries the serial number mentioned previously and the legend "Finder inform Navy, Coastguard or Police. Do not secure to or touch".

Notice No. 12. SUBMARINE CABLES AND PIPELINES
    (Similar in content to the M. Notice concerning submarine cables).

Finally it must be emphasised that the information contained in this chapter is only a brief extract of the more important information in the relevant notices up to the date of this book going to press.

Chapter Ten

Signalling

Your life or someone else's may depend upon your ability to send and receive in all mediums.

Learn all the International Signals of Distress off by heart. They are laid down in Rule 31 of the Regulations for Prevention of Collision at Sea (Chapter 6). Always have on board a copy of the International Code of Signals. The current Code is that published in 1969. It is suitable for transmission by all means of communication and intended to cater primarily for situations related to the safety of life and navigation, especially when there may be language difficulties.

The Code is divided into the General Section and the Medical Section; the latter is on green pages and each section has its own index.

The methods of signalling follow;

(*a*) Flag Signalling, the flags used being those shown in Fig. 10.1.
(*b*) Flashing light signalling.
(*c*) Sound signalling.
(*d*) Voice over a loud hailer.
(*e*) Radiotelegraphy (W/T).
(*f*) Radiotelephony (R/T).
(*g*) Signalling by hand flags or arms
      (i) by Semaphore.
      (ii) by Morse.
(*g*) is the only method for which no equipment is needed although a coloured rag or a cap in each hand makes your signal seen more easily.

Flag Signalling

Calling: If you do not identify the addressee, the signal will be understood as addressed to all stations in sight.

Answering: Code or answering pendant to the dip when signal seen; close up when understood. Repeat for each hoist transmitted.

End of Message: Code pendant singly after last hoist of text.

INTERNATIONAL
CODE OF SIGNALS

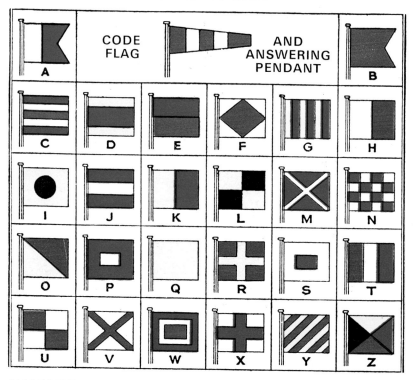

NUMERAL PENDANTS

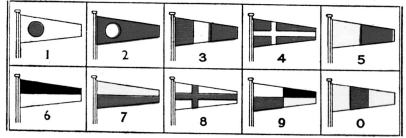

SUBSTITUTES

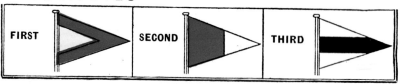

Fig 10.1

Substitutes: The first substitute repeats the first or uppermost signal flag of the group above it. The second substitute repeats the next to upper flag of the hoist and the third substitute repeats the third signal flag counting from the top. No substitute can be used more than once in the same hoist and, if the group contains flags and pendants, only refers to the class of flags immediately preceding it. The answering pendant when used as a decimal point is disregarded when assessing which substitute is required.

Spelling: Names in the text of a signal are to be spelt out. "YZ" to indicate spelling should precede the text if all in plain language.

INTERNATIONAL MORSE CODE

Letter	Character	Letter	Character	Num'l.	Character
A	· —	N	— ·	1	· — — — —
B	— · · ·	O	— — —	2	· · — — —
C	— · — ·	P	· — — ·	3	· · · — —
D	— · ·	Q	— — · —	4	· · · · —
E	·	R	· — ·	5	· · · · ·
F	· · — ·	S	· · ·	6	— · · · ·
G	— — ·	T	—	7	— — · · ·
H	· · · ·	U	· · —	8	— — — · ·
I	· ·	V	· · · —	9	— — — — ·
J	· — — —	W	· — —	0	— — — — —
K	— · —	X	— · · —		
L	· — · ·	Y	— · — —		
M	— —	Z	— — · ·		

Fig. 10.2

Flashing Light Signalling:

Use the Morse Code. See Fig. 10.2.

A bar over the letters comprising a signal means that the letters are to be made as one symbol e.g. $\overline{AR}$

Call	Identity	Text	Ending
$\overline{AA}$ $\overline{AA}$ $\overline{AA}$	de followed by name of sending vessel.	Text	$\overline{AR}$

Answering: Receiver sends "R" when message understood.

Erasing: A succession of "E"s.

Sound Signalling:

Whistle, siren, fog-horn etc.

This is a slow method and its misuse can lead to confusion.

It should be remembered that the one letter signals of the Code which are marked with an asterisk, when made by sound, may only be made in compliance with the requirements of the International Regulations for Preventing Collisions at Sea.

Radiotelephony (R/T)

Operators should comply with the current Regulations of the International Telecommunication Union.

Letters and figures are to be spelt in accordance with the spelling tables. See Fig. 10.3. When coast and ship stations are called the Call Signs or names shall be used.

Calling: Send:
Call sign of addressee not more than thrice at each call.
The group DELTA ECHO.
Call sign of the sender not more than thrice at each call.

Reply: Send:
Call sign of calling station.
DELTA ECHO.
Call sign of station called.
To call all stations send: CHARLIE QUEBEC.
If International Code Groups follow send: IN-TER-CO.
To cancel the last word or group send: KOR-REK-SHUN.
To indicate end of a transmission send: ALFA ROMEO.
To indicate receipt of a transmission send: ROMEO.
If repetition is required send: ROMEO PAPA TANGO followed, if necessary, by:
ALFA ALFA meaning all after . . .
ALFA BRAVO meaning all before . . .
BRAVO NOVEMBER meaning all between . . . and . . .
WHISKEY ALFA meaning word or group after . . .
WHISKEY BRAVO meaning word or group before . . .

PHONETIC ALPHABET

These may be used when sending code or plain language. In pronunciation the syllables in bold type are to be emphasised.

Letter	Pronunciation	Letter	Pronunciation
A	**AL** FAH	N	NO **VEM** BER
B	**BRAH** VOH	O	**OSS** CAH
C	**CHAR** LEE	P	PAH **PAH**
D	**DELL** TAH	Q	KEH **BECK**
E	**ECK** OH	R	**ROW** MEOH
F	**FOKS** TROT	S	SEE **AIR** RAH
G	GOLF	T	**TANG** GO
H	HOH **TELL**	U	**YOU** NEE FORM
I	**IN** DEEAH	V	**VIK** TAH
J	**JEW** LEE **ETT**	W	**WISS** KEY
K	**KEY** LOH	X	**ECKS** RAY
L	**LEE** MAH	Y	**YANG** KEY
M	MIKE	Z	**ZOO** LOO

FIGURE SPELLING

Each syllable should be equally emphasised.

No.	Pronunciation	No.	Pronunciation
0	NAH-DAH-ZAY-ROH	6	SOK-SEE-SIX
1	OO-NAH-WUN	7	SAY-TAY-SEVEN
2	BEES-SOH-TOO	8	OK-TOH-AIT
3	TAY-RAH-TREE	9	NO-VAY-NINER
4	KAR-TAY-FOWER	Decimal	
5	PAN-TAH-FIVE	Point	DAY-SEE-MAL
		Full Stop	STOP

Fig. 10.3

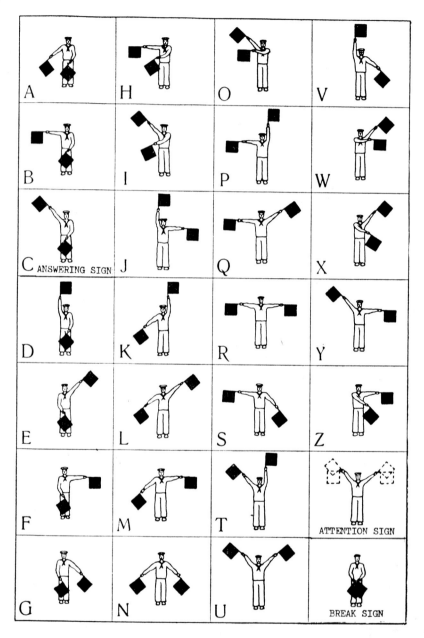

Fig. 10.4

SIGNALLING BY HAND FLAGS OR ARMS

Semaphore

The arm positions for each letter are indicated in Fig. 10.4. The shaft of the Semaphore flag should be held close up to the bunting so that the fore finger extends along it and the butt of the shaft presses against the inside of the forearm. The hand, wrist, forearm and shaft, should then be in one straight line.

When making an arm position stretch the arms to their fullest extent, keeping them in the same vertical plane as the body.

A signal by this method should always be in plain language and any numbers occurring in the signal are always to be spelt out in words.

Calling: Give the attention sign, see Fig. 10.4 or send "KI" KILO UNAONE by any method.

Answering: Hoist answering pendant to dip when attention sign sighted, and close up when ready to receive.

Receiving: Indicate receipt of each word by making the Semaphore letter "C".

End of Message: Send $\overline{\text{AR}}$.
Erasing: Send a succession of E's.

Morse Signalling by Hand Flags or Arms.

Calling: $\overline{\text{AA}}$ $\overline{\text{AA}}$ $\overline{\text{AA}}$ or address a particular station with (K2) KILO BISSOTWO by any method.

Answering: "T".

Ending: $\overline{\text{AR}}$.

Normally both arms should be used for this method but a yachtsman may find the need to hold on with one hand, in which case one arm may be used to transmit.
The attitudes showing the different symbols are in Fig. 10.5. They should be practised, extending the arms to their full extent in the same vertical plane as the body.

MORSE SIGNALLING BY HAND FLAGS OR ARMS

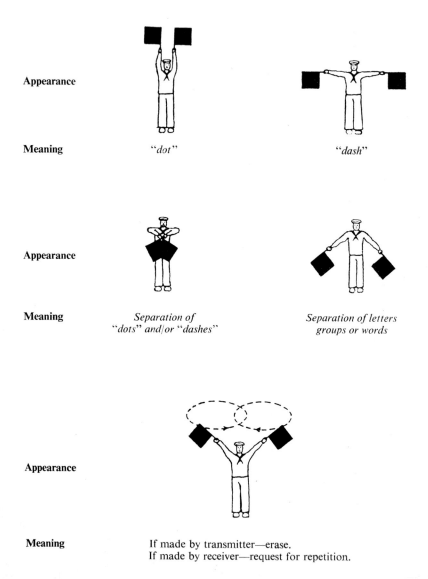

Appearance

Meaning   *"dot"*   *"dash"*

Appearance

Meaning   *Separation of*   *Separation of letters*
                 "dots" and/or "dashes"   *groups or words*

Appearance

Meaning   If made by transmitter—erase.
                     If made by receiver—request for repetition.

Fig. 10.5

SINGLE LETTER SIGNALS BY FLAG, LIGHT, OR SOUND

The most important Code signals of all—the single letter signals—consist of Very Urgent signals or those in common use. Seamen should know these by heart, so that there may be no hesitation in acting on them.

The following may be made by any method of signalling, but those marked (*) when made by sound may only be made in compliance with the International Regulations for Preventing Collisions at Sea, Rules 15 and 28.

A	· —	I have a diver down; keep well clear at slow speed.
B	— · · ·	I am taking in, or discharging, or carrying dangerous goods.
C	— · — ·	Yes (affirmative or "The significance of the previous group should be read in the affirmative").
*D	— · ·	Keep clear of me—I am manoeuvring with difficulty.
*E	·	I am altering my course to starboard.
F	· · — ·	I am disabled. Communicate with me.
G	— — ·	I require a Pilot. When made by fishing vessels operating in close proximity on the fishing grounds it means: "I am hauling nets".
*H	· · · ·	I have a Pilot on board.
*I	· ·	I am altering my course to port.
J	· — — —	I am on fire and have dangerous cargo on board: keep well clear of me.
K	— · —	I wish to communicate with you.
L	· — · ·	You should stop your vessel instantly.
M	— —	My vessel is stopped and making no way through the water.
N	— ·	No (negative or "The significance of the previous group should be read in the negative"). This signal may be given only visually or by sound. For voice or radio transmission the signal should be "No".
O	— — —	Man overboard.
P	· — — ·	In Harbour (Blue Peter) All persons should report on board as the vessel is about to proceed to sea. (Note.—To be hoisted at the foremast head). At Sea. It may be used by fishing vessels to mean "My nets have come fast upon an obstruction".
Q	— — · —	My vessel is healthy and I request free pratique.
‡R	· — ·	
*S	· · ·	My engines are going astern.
*T	—	Keep clear of me; I am engaged in pair trawling.
U	· · —	You are running into danger.
V	· · · —	I require assistance.
W	· — —	I require medical assistance.
X	— · · —	Stop carrying out your intentions and watch for my signals.
Y	— · — —	I am dragging my anchor.
Z	— — · ·	I require a tug. When made by fishing vessels operating in close proximity on the fishing grounds it means: "I am shooting nets".

‡Single letter Signal R has so far not been allocated a Signal meaning as this already has a meaning in Rule 15 of the collision Regulations.

SINGLE LETTER SIGNALS WITH COMPLEMENTS

To signal an AZIMUTH or Bearing hoist: A with three numerals.
  Course: C with three numerals.
  Distance in nautical miles: R with one or more numerals.
  Latitude: L with four numerals.
  In this signal the *first* two numerals denote *degrees* and the rest minutes.
  Longitude: G with four or five numerals.
  In this signal the *last* two numerals denote minutes and the rest degrees.
  Speed in knots: S with one or more numerals.
  Speed in kilometres per hour: V with one or more numerals.
  Date: D with two, four or six numerals.
  In the next two signals the first two numerals denote hours and the rest minutes.
  GMT: Z with four numerals.
  Local Time: T with four numerals.

In the Department of Trade & Industry examination you will be required to send and receive signals in the Morse code using a flash lamp at up to six words a minute and in British Semaphore up to eight words a minute. The syllabus includes the International Code of Signals; therefore you should study the layout and contents of the Code Book which may be made available to you by the Examiner for the purpose of coding or decoding a message.

THE ADMIRALTY LIST OF RADIO SIGNALS

The various Volumes under this title should be perused with diligence. They contain a wealth of information relating to Coastal Radio Stations, Radio Direction Finding Beacons, Medical Advice by Radio, Radar Beacons, Weather Messages, Time Signals and Position Fixing Systems. They are kept up-to-date by corrections notified in Notices to Mariners.

Chapter Eleven

Precautionary
& Emergency Procedure

Gybing

This may be defined as bringing the wind from one quarter to the other round the stern.
It can happen accidentally because of a sudden squall or inattentive steering.
An accidental gybe can be of great danger to the sailorman.
The boom can send crew overboard or might even break. You might part a backstay, halyard or sheet, or even be dismasted.
When running before the wind guy your boom forward, outside everything, to a suitable place, through a fairlead if necessary. This will act as a check but an accidental gybe must be avoided by alert steering. Be prepared to down helm immediately the mainsail leach tends to lift.

Pooping and Broaching-to

A following sea overtaking you can be upset by your own wake so that it breaks over your stern and may fill you. This is known as being pooped.
Broaching-to is being forced broadside into a trough and can happen when running down the advance side of a steep wave. The bow goes under and the stern is lifted and carried on. The boat is then twisted too much for your rudder to cope with. The sea may break over you, and put you on your beam ends or cause a capsize.
When running before the sea NEVER RUN TOO LONG. Bring her round and heave to before it is too late. If you have left it too late, or for some reason it is imperative that you run on, do it under easy sail and pay out a mooring rope, or better still a sea anchor, over the stern.

Heaving-to

This is done in bad weather to stop the boat trying to smash through the seas. The aim is to take the seas from ahead easily, and keep the decks dry. Shorten sail right down to the storm jib, with reefed mainsail and back the jib to weather. Lash your tiller to leeward, leaving some movement in it and lie with the wind about four points on the bow. Alternatively, put a sea anchor out forward, and in very bad weather attach a vegetable oil bag. This will create a slick to windward and prevent the seas from breaking.

Sea Anchor

If you sail offshore you should have one. It consists of a conical shaped canvas bag wide open at one end with a much smaller hole at its apex. A rough guide to size is that the open end should have a diameter of one inch for each foot length of your boat. The larger end must have a means of keeping it open and have a bridle on it to which the hawser is bent. The hawser should be at least three times the length of your boat. To the smaller end is attached a smaller or tripping line which should be a few fathoms longer than the hawser. An oil bag may be run out to the sea anchor by taking your jib halyard block and halyard down and attaching the block near the anchor end of the hawser.

Put the sea anchor out over the weather bow. Watch out for chafing of the hawser at the fairlead. Make the tripping line fast but slack. To take in the sea anchor, slack the hawser easily until the weight comes on the tripping line then haul in small end first.

The sea anchor might also be used approaching the land under sail and before the wind by putting it out over the stern to act as a brake. The tripping line used sensibly will release the brake as necessary.

More usually warps over the stern would be safer.

If it is found necessary to beach, the safety way is to back in with the anchor over the bow dredging (or use the sea anchor).

Broken rigging

If your *forestay* parts put the boat before the wind. Lower your jib and take the halyard to the stem as a temporary measure. Make a new forestay with the best line you have and make for port. If you are close to shoals or shore, anchor.

If your *backstay* carries away, tack the boat or gybe her to bring the wind on her other side. Lower your jib and proceed as for the forestay.

If your *halyard* parts bring the boat to the wind hauling in on your sheet. Gather in the sail. Reeve off a new halyard, make it fast, then hoist away and re-set your sail.

If your *boom topping lift* carries away bring her to the wind and haul in on the sheet. Get the boom on to the lee quarter, lash it there and lower the sail until you can reeve off a new topping lift.

If your *mainsheet* parts bring her to the wind, top the boom with the topping lift then get it inboard. Reeve a new sheet or lower mainsail and boom and set a trysail to take you to port.

If you are *dismasted* in heavy weather the broken gear will be in the sea alongside and in danger of holeing your boat. Cut it away making sure to keep the forestay or shrouds so that the boat will ride to the gear as to a sea anchor. If you are on a lee shore anchor as soon as possible, but in open water try to ride out the bad weather and effect a jury rig.

Man Overboard

If running before the wind throw a lifebuoy, shout Man Overboard and gybe. Keep a lookout on the man in the water. Bring her round on to the tack that will put the man on the weather bow and stand towards him. Get near enough to throw a line and pick the man up on the weather bow, putting the tiller down to bring the boat to the wind as you come up with him.

In heavy weather a gybe may be more than you care to risk in which case you must put your tiller down and bring her close hauled, then tack towards him. Careful judgment is needed here as, if you bring her close hauled too soon, you may get too far to windward and cause much delay by having to run to leeward and work back to windward again.

If a man goes overboard at night note your compass heading and keep a log of all your movements as you may have difficulty finding him. It is possible that you may have no success until daylight, if he can survive until then, and at that time you will want to be sure that you are searching the right area.

Capsizing

Your emergency drill should be such that in the event of a capsize your crew will stay with the boat. They will at least have something to hold on to and the boat, though upturned, is more likely to be spotted by rescuers than a single head in the water. If you have lashed your watertight container of distress signals by means of a long lanyard there is a good chance that it will float free and they may be the means of initiating your rescue. If you have foolishly stowed the container away in a locker you may be able to get it by removing your lifejacket and diving under the boat but this should be a desperate measure and to be avoided by not closing it away in the first place. If your boat is one which you are unlikely to be able to right, release your inflatable liferaft and get in to it until rescued.

Running aground

In a river on a rising tide lower your sails if you are on a lee shore. Run out your anchor and haul off into deeper water as the tide rises, having searched for damage and made sure that she is not taking or will not take in water. On a falling tide you must act immediately and quickly. In a yacht and all wearing lifejackets the quickest way to get her off may be for all to go overboard and push. The loss of weight may lighten her sufficiently for this method to succeed but it may be advisable to lower your sails before trying.

On an offshore shoal you may act in a similar manner to the above but if you do not succeed in getting her off before the tide rises you must remember your more open position should the weather deteriorate and have your liferaft ready should the worst happen.

Beaching

If you have reached a state where you have decided to beach your boat great care must be used. You must endeavour to choose a sandy stretch clear of any rock or other obstructions and be aware that your greatest danger is that of broaching-to.

If you have to bring her in through broken sea or surf, get her to seaward of the stretch of beach you have chosen and lower her sails and mast before entering any broken water, and prepare your oars for rowing. Stream your sea anchor out over the bow to help keep her head to sea and back her in keeping her head to the sea by using the oars as necessary.

If the beach is a flat one keep straight before the sea until she takes the ground when the crew should jump out to lighten her and drag her in.

If the beach is steep and help can be seen ready and waiting it may be better in the act of landing to turn her broadside on to the surf so that she is thrown broadside up the beach.

Precautions entering harbour

Study the Pilot Book for the area and have a large scale chart available. See that your sails, if any, are ready to lower, with the halyards ready for running. Have your anchor ready for letting go and a line to make fast to a buoy, if such is your berth. Otherwise have sufficient mooring lines, springs and fenders ready, together with heaving lines. Have your leadline ready and hand your patent log if you have been using one.

If you are sailing in watch out for any high cliffs or buildings which may steal your wind and remember that at many harbours there is a very strong run of tide across the entrance

Form CG66

As a final word, obtain a supply of this Form from the Coastguard.

Before each passage complete one and hand it to the Coastguard. It will describe your vessel and intentions. Do not forget to report your arrival at your destination, or if you put in to an intermediate haven. Such a lapse of memory may result in the whole Air-Sea Rescue Organisation being alerted unnecessarily.

Appendix

The oral examinations on Seamanship in the syllabuses for Certificate of Competency as Yacht Master, both Coastal and Ocean, are virtually the same.

Details of the oral examination are given below:

(1) Standing and running rigging. Blocks, purchases and tackles. Cordage and its use and care. Bends, hitches, knots, splices and seizings. Passing stoppers.

(2) Use of hand lead line.

(3) Handling of sailing boats (fore and aft rig). Bending, setting and taking in sail. Management of boats under oars and sails and in heavy weather. Beaching and landing. Coming alongside under oars or sail.

(4) Handling of power boats. Effects of propellers on the steering of a boat, stopping and going astern. Manoeuvring. Turning circles, effect of current, wind, sea, shallows and draught. Turning a boat short round. Man overboard.

(5) Coming alongside and securing, including berths that dry out. Making fast to a buoy. Anchoring. Leaving a wharf in a tideway. Use of head ropes, breast ropes and springs.

(6) Navigation in fog.

(7) A knowledge of the use of lifesaving appliances with particular reference to those required for yachts. Use of rocket apparatus and breeches buoy. Line throwing rockets.

(8) A knowledge of the use of fire extinguishing appliances with particular reference to those required to be carried by yachts. Precautions to be taken to prevent outbreaks of fire.

(9) A full knowledge of the content and application of the Collision Regulations. Candidates will be placed in the position of handling a yacht under sail.

(10) Duties in case of collision.

(11) Distress and pilot signals; penalties for misuse.

(12) British uniform system of buoyage; wreck marking systems.

(13) A knowledge of the contents of the Department of Trade and Industry Merchant Shipping Notices, limited to those applying to small craft. A knowledge of the use of form CG66. The use of Admiralty Notices to Mariners. An outline knowledge of the contents of pilot books. The use of the Admiralty List of Radio Signals.

(14) To read an aneroid barometer.

(15) To use a sextant for taking vertical and horizontal angles; and (in the case of the Ocean Certificate only) to read a sextant on and off the arc.

(16) To find the index error of a sextant.

(17) A knowledge of the type of weather messages broadcast by the BBC which are available for shipping.

INDEX